Monkey Flip

Brian Webster and Kathy Garrett

Published by Idea Works, LTD
by Brian Webster

Layout by
Gwen Frederickson

Edited by
Kris Yankee

Publishing Coordination by
Tim Trinka

Printed in the United States of America

Cover: Christopher Webster

To Christopher

CHAPTER ONE

"Chris! Chriiis! Christopher! I have been calling you for ten minutes! If you don't jump out of bed now you're going to be late for school!"

Even though I've heard this about a thousand times, it takes me a minute to understand what my mom is saying and why she's poking me. I blink at her.

"Chris," she says again, this time quietly because she sees I'm awake, "Warren's not just around the block like Kennedy." She walks to the window and snaps the shades up. The sudden sunlight does not help my mood.

"Not going," I tell her, trying to sound definite.

"Yes, you are." She uses her serious voice when she yanks the covers off me.

"Nope. Not going. You don't know what it's like to go to a different school and try to make new friends," I mumble.

"I do too! It's hard. Really hard. But it's worth it. Besides, Warren's a better fit for you. They have the services you need there," my mom adds sounding more like she's talking to herself than me.

"'Services.' Great. I need 'Services.' I still don't know why we couldn't wait until next year."

"Honey, we've been through this. It's got the services, the program – it's got what you need to do well in school. If we wait until next year, you might not be able to get in."

She's got me cornered, but I'm not ready to give in. I pull the covers over my head. A weak move I know, but it's all I can think of this early in the morning.

"You can't hide, Chris," she says yanking the covers off of me again.

"But I want to," I say. I make her wait before I give it one last pathetic attempt. My head is back under the covers. I remember when I was little I'd hide under the bed thinking it was the greatest hiding place in the world. I wish there was a place I could hide and no one would find me.

"Oh, honestly, Chris, sometimes you're just like my second graders," she says.

"Thanks a lot. Look, Mom, I got lost at Kennedy. Warren's twice as big. I'll feel like a rat in a giant maze."

"Honey, I don't have time for this." I've heard that before too. I know it's over. She pulls the covers off my head. "Cereal's on the table," she says and she's gone.

"This sucks," I whisper to the poster of Tony Hawk hanging on the back of the door she just closed. My alarm clock buzzes like a chainsaw on the table next to my bed. I slam my fist on it as is my usual way of turning it off, and knock over the picture of my dad and me with my first bass I caught when I was seven. "Yep, this sucks."

Sucky or not, I know my mom is through messing around. I pull on some pants from the floor and my "Joe's Pizza" t-shirt and head downstairs. Sure enough, there's the cereal. In my final, and, I admit, lame, act of rebellion I ignore the cereal and instead grab a piece of pizza from the fridge. Then I grab my backpack, my lunch, and my board, toss the board down the four back steps, jump on it and make my way at first fast and then slowly to Warren Middle School, home of the "Special Services."

CHAPTER TWO

Just as I finish a long, sweet grind along a bench and then the curb, I feel Warren Middle's gigantic presence. I wonder how I can incorporate the massive flagpole into a trick. Could I somehow go up or around the pole? The base is sort of a cement square with steps, so that's easy, but the steel pole won't work for anything I know how to do. My inventing is interrupted by the bell which anyone, new kid or not, knows it's time to head in. Kids are everywhere, talking loud, laughing, running, pushing. Everyone seems to know everyone else, and everyone seems to know exactly where they're going. Everyone except me, of course.

The halls are crowded, but I'm able to get around pretty good on my board. The classroom numbers don't seem like they're in order, but I know they must be. I keep looking at the half sheet of paper in my hand and the black numbers on the classroom doors, trying to keep my mumbling to myself to a minimum. Kids jostle me and I hear someone practically yell, "Seriously? A skateboard? That kid can't skateboard in here!" Just when I think I've found it, I realize that the numbers on the door aren't the numbers on the paper. I hate this. In my old school I had all the classrooms memorized. No need to compare them to any paper. The halls are loud but getting quieter as all the other kids easily find their classes. I am absolutely not going to ask anyone for help, but I'm getting desperate. Finally, when it's just me and some kid with a clipboard in the hall, room 301A is right in front of me, clear as a bell. "Aha!" I accidentally say out loud and glide, victorious into room 301A.

"Yes?" The first thing I notice is that the teacher is wearing a bowtie. He also has those round professor glasses. He's also really short, but most everyone is shorter than me when I'm on my board. He looks like the kind of person who's never happy.

"Uh, is this English? Room 103A?" I know everyone in the room is staring at me, but I'm trying real hard not to look at all the faces looking at me.

"Close," Professor Bowtie says.

I got it wrong? Wait. I look at my paper again, and see - of course. Professor Bowtie points to the chalkboard where his name "Mr. Hess" and "English Room 301A" are written in huge letters. I look back at the paper and I don't get it. I look back at the board and then at the paper again. I hear, "It ain't rocket science, Loser" from someone, and then I do get it: 103, 301. "Oh yeah, I see it now," I say looking at Mr. Hess.

"Very good," Mr. Hess says. I can't tell if he's being a jerk or not. "I don't recognize you, which means that you must be…" he asks.

"Chris Reynolds?" Now I can definitely feel everyone staring at me, more than ready to crack up at the idiot who can't read room numbers. "I'm new."

"Duh! What a dork!" some kid says. I think it's the same kid talking, but I still haven't looked around.

"Well Mr. Reynolds, take a seat. And tomorrow you will be a little earlier, yes?"

"Yes sir," I nod and roll over to the only empty seat in the class, right in front, between a girl with long brown hair and a huge, smirking kid.

"And in my classroom, Mr. Reynolds, and I dare say in any classroom, we do not wheel our way around the school."

"Oh yeah, sorry. I was in a hurry, I guess, kinda got lost," I know that I sound like a complete idiot. The big kid next to me chuckles and mutters something I can't hear but I know it's got something to do with what a genius I am. I also know that this is the kid who has already called me a loser and a dork. Great.

"Ok class, let's return to what we were doing. Robert Frost. The name of the poem is 'The Trial by Existence'. As you know – or should know by now – Frost was an unsuccessful farmer." Mr. Hess starts pacing the front of the room, holding a book talking about Frost. I think this might be ok as I know a lot of Frost's poems because of my dad, but then I feel the big kid's eyes on me. I look over at him quickly and see he's drawn a picture of a kid with big buck teeth, crazy eyes and a dunce cap on his head, riding a skateboard. "Duh?" is in a bubble coming out of his mouth. Mr. Hess notices none of this. He's just going on about Frost. I'm trying really hard to listen, well maybe not listen, but to disappear before this kid makes me do something I know I'll regret, but I can't get my board to stop rolling out from under my desk and, like an idiot, it does not occur to me to turn it over.

"Mr. Reynolds, do you suppose you could be a little quieter?" Mr. Hess is at the front of my desk before I even notice he's stopped rambling about Frost, and he sounds mad.

"Yes, sir, sorry." About five seconds later I accidentally kick my board sending it rolling again. The chuckling is quickly turning to out and out laughing, making Mr. Hess talk louder.

"And perhaps he is best known for his poem 'The Road Not Taken' and for being poet laureate under John F. Kennedy." Mr. Hess quiets down as I finally flip my board over and sit up trying to look eager. "In fact, at Kennedy's request, Frost became the first poet ever to read at a presidential inauguration which has since become the tradition at presidential inaugurations."

I kick my feet back, forgetting about my board, and out it

goes again, sliding under the seat behind me. "What a joke," the kid next to me says, this time loud.

"Buzz off." Weak, I know, but I gotta say something.

"Excuse me, Mr. Reynolds?" Mr. Hess is definitely mad, really mad. He's standing right in front of me again. He's closed the book and is staring at me, hand on his hips.

"No I wasn't talking to you, I was —"

"I had planned to have Mr. Parks read the poem for us, but perhaps you would like to, Mr. Reynolds."

"Uh." Just when I thought things couldn't get worse. Reading out loud in front of a class is hands down one of the most embarrassing things I'm ever asked to do. And I know this from years, literally years, of experience. Doesn't matter how much I know about Frost or poetry or anything at all really. I would rather stick a fork in my neck than read out loud in front of other people.

"Come on now. The class is waiting. We only have forty-seven minute periods in this school. You have taken up more than your share of these precious few minutes with your disruptions. I think it only fitting that you help the class focus on the task at hand," Mr. Hess says opening his book and handing it to me. "Page 78 'The Trial of Existence.' If you please, Mr. Reynolds."

Of course I start to try to read before I realize that the book is upside down. And of course I hear a bunch of people laugh. Maybe I'm cured. I give it a go: "Even the dravest that are slain…" I say and immediately feel sweaty.

"Bravest."

"Huh?"

"'Even the bravest that are slain,' Mr. Reynolds. It's 'bravest' not 'dravest'. You said 'dravest'," Mr. Hess says, already losing patience.

"Oh yeah." I gotta get this over with as fast as possible. "'Even the bravest that are slain. Shall not…besettle their supper.'" Now the kids are howling, actually howling with laughter. I close the book and wish for a hole to open up under my desk.

"Mr. Reynolds, are you trying to be funny? Because if you are, you're too late. We've already covered comedy in this class. I wouldn't think you'd want to make such a bad impression your first day in a new school."

I looked up the word "livid" once. Turns out it's a color, like purple. Mr. Hess is purple right now. I get why people say "I'm livid!" when someone gets super angry. He's livid and I know I'm beet red. Before I have a chance to think of something to say, the big kid next to me raises his hand.

"Yes, Mr. Parks?"

"Mr. Hess, I'm afraid Mr. Reynolds has skated into the wrong class."

I can tell this dude isn't trying to be helpful, not with that stupid grin on his face.

"Yeah, the remedial room is two doors down." Some kid in the back says.

"Right. It's no problem, Mr. Hess, I'd be happy to help Mr. Reynolds find the room." Then he stands up and walks stiff-legged and spastic toward the door, which makes most of the other kids howl again. He and I aren't gonna get along. That I know.

"Mr. Parks, sit down. Unless of course, you want to sashay yourself down to the principal's office. She hasn't seen you yet today. As for you, Mr. Reynolds, I don't think you'd like the reputation of a trouble maker so early in your career at Warren Middle School." Mr. Hess takes a deep breath and pushes up his glasses. "Now then," he says and takes the book back from me.

I see the Parks kid point to the other loud-mouth in the back of the room and give an air high five. Then I see the girl with the long hair cross her arms fast and hard. She's not laughing. She looks mad, or maybe she's livid. This is all happening so fast I have no clear idea how things got so bad so quickly. I'm not usually a principal's office kid, but here, on my first day, I almost land myself there. I try to concentrate again as Mr. Hess starts talking about Frost.

"Miss Benson, do you think you could manage to read the first stanza of Frost's poem?" Mr. Hess asks, and a girl sitting near the windows perks up. She's obviously the teacher's pet. Not so different from my old school, or any school probably. Miss Benson pops out of her chair like someone goosed her and practically runs to the front of the room where she reads, perfectly of course:

> "'Even the bravest that are slain
> Shall not dissemble their surprise
> On waking to find valor reign,
> Even as on earth, in paradise;
> And where they sought without the sword
> Wide fields of asphodel fore'er,
> To find that the utmost reward
> Of daring should be still to dare.'
>
> From the poem 'The Trial by Existence' by Robert Frost."

As she reads I try my best to listen to the words, but about halfway through I hear "Hey! Psst!" from the long haired girl. I look and she mouths "Don't worry about it," and smiles quickly. Before I can smile back, she's looking at her notebook as if nothing happened. Once again, I feel as if I am the only one who has no idea what is going on.

CHAPTER THREE

After English there was Science and then Gym. All these went ok – none as bad as English. Gym of course was the best. I'm pretty good at whatever sport I try. And then, finally, lunch – potentially another sticky 40 minutes. At the door to the cafeteria, I try to look for a place to sit without looking like I'm looking for a place to sit. It's loud like the cafeteria at my old school. Some kids sit huddled together looking like they're plotting something, some kids laugh their heads off showing each other their half chewed mouths of food, and some kids read while they eat. I figure the best thing to do is to tune everyone else out. I pretend that it's fine with me if I eat lunch alone. Doesn't bother me a bit, nope, everything is just fiine I put on my headphones, head to the nearest table with a spot open, and eat the leftover pizza I brought from home. Just as I'm getting into the music, the long-haired girl stands at the opposite side of the table mouthing something to me.

"Oh! Sorry! What did you say?" I whip off my headphones.

"I said, 'Can I sit down?'"

"Sit? Yeah, of course."

"How's your first day going?" she asks like we're old friends or something.

"Me? Fine I guess, well, except for first hour. Why?" She's not making me feel like a genius here. I have no idea what she wants.

"Well, I wanted to apologize." She doesn't seem to notice how awkward this is.

"Apologize? For what?"

"The other kids. In Mr. Hess' class. They're pretty rude," she says, unfolding her napkin and putting it on her lap. Who brings a napkin in a school lunch, I wonder.

"Aw, that's all right. No big deal," I say. Why would she apologize for them?

"Well, I know it sounds weird, but I'm in the Warren Welcomers. We try to make sure new students feel comfortable here, you know, included like. I know what it's like moving to a new school, especially in mid-year," she says. She doesn't seem to feel awkward. She just seems really nice.

"Oh, yeah. Thanks." So now I've gone from feeling clueless to feeling, well, I'm not sure. This girl is possibly the prettiest girl I have ever said two words to.

"Does your family move a lot?" she asks right before she takes a bite of sandwich. I suddenly notice that she sat down and that we're eating lunch together.

"Huh? Uh, no. No. Always lived here," I mumble, for once regretting that I don't have a napkin to wipe my mouth.

"You just moved to a new house then. That's cool."

"No, same house." I really don't want to explain why I'm at Warren.

"Oh sorry. I probably ask way too many questions. My family's moved around a lot. My father was in the military, so yeah..." she says, taking a sip of milk.

"Was?" I ask.

"Yeah. He's got a civilian job now, so we've been in the same house for two years. It's great actually. It gets tiring moving around all the time."

"Yeah." I seriously have to work on my conversation skills.

"I kind of wanted to apologize for Wheeler," she says quieting a little.

"Wheeler?"

"Frank Parks, or 'Mr. Parks' as Mr. Hess would say. The one who was giving you the hardest time. You know, the kid who was sitting next to you." She imitates Parks' spaz impression and we both laugh. "It's not really funny. No one should be making fun of people with disabilities. I mean, I don't think you have a disability, not that there'd be anything wrong with it if you did – I just think it's rude no matter who or what or…"

It's nice to see someone else stumble over words for a change.

She takes a deep breath. "I mean, if I walked into a class on my first day and the teacher asked me to read out loud in front of a bunch of kids I don't know, I'd be a basket case," she says making her eyes go real big.

I nod, grateful for the understanding. "Yeah, I probably looked like a basket case," I say smiling.

"I think you handled it pretty well actually. Besides, I think Wheeler was kind of sizing you up."

"Sizing me up? Why bother? He's way bigger than me."

"No, it's not to fight so much as skate. Wheeler's a competitive skateboarder. I think that's why he was messing with you. He saw you with your board and sees you as competition. He's won lots of trophies and stuff. Even money. And he doesn't like to lose. He just wanted to make sure that you aren't going to be a threat," she says. "Super insecure if you ask me."

"I don't know about insecure," I say and then think for a minute. "But me? A threat? Fat chance. Tell him he doesn't have to worry about me. I've never competed in my life. I just skate for fun and to get around. It's the only way I can get around. I've got no bike and it's not like my mom's going to drive me everyplace."

And then the girl with the long brown hair smiles big, right at me. "Oh, I completely forgot." She sticks her hand out at me and says "My name's Jennifer. Jen to my friends. Call me Jen."

I instantly grab her hand to shake it and smear her with pizza sauce. Smooth, real smooth.

"Oh! Sorry! I didn't know…"

But she just laughs, looks at her hand and suddenly gets this fake-serious look and says "'Out, damned spot! Out, I say!— One: two: why, then, 'tis time to do't.—Hell is murky!—Fie, my lord, fie! a soldier, and afeard?'" She wipes her hand on a napkin and says "*Macbeth* Act 5, Scene 1 lines 35-37. Lady Macbeth."

"I know," I tell her, "*Othello*'s my favorite, but I really like the witches in *Macbeth*," I say, and she stares back at me.

"You do?"

"Yeah, my dad taught English in college. Poetry, actually. Well, he was a poet too. At least he tried to be," I tell her as she hands me a napkin so I can wipe off my hand.

"I always get extras," she says. "It's because I have two younger siblings and do a lot of babysitting. You can never have too many paper napkins." I'm smiling, but she looks a little, well, embarrassed maybe. Her face is kind of red and blotchy. "That's kind of crazy that you know Shakespeare."

"Crazy? Why? Cuz I'm a dork?" I ask.

"No, no! I don't think you're a dork, not at all. It's just that not a lot of kids here know Shakespeare let alone like it. I'm just surprised anyone here knows Shakespeare," Jen says looking embarrassed.

"Maybe we're both dorks," I say.

"Ha! Maybe," she says and then asks after an awkward pause, "So, do you have brothers and sisters?"

"No, just me. And my mom."

She looks up at me smiling, but then quickly frowns looking at something behind me.

"Making new friends, Jen? That's nice of you to make friends with the moron." It's Frank Parks, or 'Wheeler' as I guess everyone calls him. Still being a jerk apparently.

"I'm a member of the Warren Welcomers, Frank, remember? We try to make new students feel welcome? Do you know what that means?" She looks as if she just might punch him.

"Oh, right. What's it called again? 'Welcome Wagon'? 'Welcome Warriors'? 'Welcome Wenches'? It's Welcome something, I know that." Then he sticks his hand out toward me. "My name's Wheeler."

I shake it more like a reaction than a decision. After about five seconds, Wheeler won't let go and starts squeezing.

"What kind of a handshake is this? Ya gotta grip harder, Reynolds. Give me your best man handshake."

Then we get in this stupid contest of who can crush whose hand, and I'm losing.

"Like this, Reynolds, ya gotta be firm, show the world you mean business." And then he squeezes until I can feel all the little bones in my hand start to look for somewhere else to go. I can't help it, my eyes start watering.

"Cut it out, Frank," Jen says, staring at Wheeler.

"You used to call me Wheeler," he says without breaking his grip on my crumpled hand.

"That was then, this is now," Jen says through her gritted teeth. "Don't be a jerk."

Wheeler finally lets go and I try not to crumble to the floor. "Does Mr. Reynolds have a first name?" Wheeler asks like nothing's happened.

"Chris." I do my best not to whimper.

"This is Vert. Grinder." I just now notice two goons on either side of Wheeler. One of them, Vert I guess, is the kid from the back of the class who found Wheeler's jokes so hilarious. Both of Wheeler's friends offer to shake hands.

"Actually I was just leaving," I say, turning to go, but Wheeler's shoulder bumps me right into this African-American lady whose tray flips up, splattering her lunch all over the front of her. Wheeler's friends practically collapse trying to hide their laughing. Before I can say anything, Wheeler is all polite: "Ah jeez, sorry, Ms. James. My friend here, Chris, Chris Reynolds, is new here and just a little clumsy. I hope you won't be too upset with my new friend."

I cannot stand this kid. Definitely cannot stand him. Jen is practically falling over the table trying to get to Ms. James.

"Here let me help you, Ms. James. I'm sure it was an accident. I'm so sorry," Jen says, using all her extra napkins on Ms. James' suit.

"Oh, that's all right, Jen. Just one of those days." Ms. James looks at me, and I can't believe it, but she says, "Nice to meet you Chris. I'm sure we'll be running into each other again, so to speak."

"I, uh –"

"Don't worry about it, Chris, really. Come referendum time, the voters treat us much worse. If you'll excuse me," Ms. James says and he heads off, still wiping mashed potatoes and gravy from her suit.

"You're such a jerk!" Jen hisses at Wheeler.

"Oh, come on, Jen. It was an accident, just like you said."

"Bull," Jen says. Then she grabs my arm and starts to pull me out of the cafeteria.

After we walk down the hall a little ways, Jen takes a deep breath and says "I'm so sorry about that. You must be having the worst first day ever."

"You don't need to apologize for stuff other people do." I tell her.

"You're right, sor- I mean, you're right," Jen takes a deep breath and smiles. "I'll show you around a little before the next bell rings."

Wheeler and his buddies are behind us and I hear Wheeler say "Hey, Jen, wait up."

"Stop following me, Frank. If you think doing stuff like that is going to make me want to go back with you, forget it!" Jen yells over her shoulder. I am unclear as to exactly what's happening, but I'm beginning to get an idea.

CHAPTER FOUR

After a couple of weeks of doing my best to avoid Wheeler and his goons by sitting as far away from them as possible, and by coming into class right when the bell rings and leaving the second it rings again, one day I'm carrying my board from my locker through the double doors and I toss it down the steps to the sidewalk in front. As usual, I don't hang around after school. I figure if I get outside as soon as I can after the last bell rings, the chances of me running into Wheeler are less. He'll be too busy showing off or messing with some other kid to get out of school quickly.

This time, though, I hear music coming from the gym as I skate by. I double back. The door is held open just a little with a rock, so I look through the window in the door to see what's going on. I'm really not planning on staying long, but then I see Jen on a balance beam, she's actually on her hands on a balance beam. I mean she's perfectly still up there upside down and she's scissoring her legs like it's the easiest thing in the world. Wow. Then my face gets crushed against the window.

"What are you looking at, Retard?" I hear Wheeler's voice from behind.

It's a little garbled, but I manage: "Right now I'm looking at a door."

"Friggin' peeping Tom." I can't see him, but I'm thinking this time it's the Vert kid talking.

"You may not know this, New Boy, but Jen is a special friend of mine and I'm not too keen with other guys spending time with her, ok?" Wheeler says and lets go of the back of my head. Slowly my vision straightens out.

"Ok? You hear me, Loser?"

I'm nodding and moving my face around to get it back to normal. "Yeah, I heard."

"Besides, she's a tease. She'll come on to you like she's interested, then poof. She's gone."

He's looking at me like I'm supposed to react or something, but I got nothing. I just look at him and shrug.

"Suddenly you're just another 'friend,' like half the guys in the school," Wheeler adds making air quotes and sneering.

Looks to me like somebody's a little grumpy, had his little shriveled heart broken, but I keep my mouth shut and just nod.

"You don't know nothing about her – nothing. If I were you, I'd just leave her alone. Just a warning." Wheeler's pointing his finger right at my forehead.

I nod again trying hard not to say anything that will get my face smashed in, but it's not easy. Tough guy Vert kicks my board out from under my feet and I go down.

"What the -?" are the first words I manage.

"Oops. Sorry, Dude. I just wanted to check out your board." Vert's holding my board and showing it to Wheeler. Grinder leans in to see it too. "I think he needs a new board. This one has scratches on it. Cute stickers though. To each his own," Vert says then drops the board on its nose.

"Jeez Vert, be nice. The Welcome Wenches won't like this," Wheeler smiles and curtsies at me.

I get back up and we all look into the gym when we hear Jen yell "Frank!" She's heading toward us and she looks pissed. I turn my board, grab my back pack and clock Vert squarely in the jaw and then I take off.

"Crap!" I hear Wheeler yell, and then I hear the sound of boards hitting the pavement and I know I gotta step on the gas. I don't know the layout of the school grounds like I should because I get out and go home as fast as I can, but these guys know it, and before I can get free of the grounds I've been doubled back toward the gym which leaves me no choice but to go inside. I have the feeling this is not going to end well. All three are behind me, taking the hallway turns without a problem. I hairpin it into the closest open door.

They don't make the turn so I stop a second. I hear them stop too I turn my head to listen and then I hear Wheeler say "We'll let him face the Hydra."

Suddenly there's screaming from inside the room I'm in. I spin my head around but instantly wish I hadn't. "Oh boy," I mutter to myself, and then I try really hard not to see girls, some with all their clothes on, some with nothing but a towel on who are doing the screaming.

"This is not good, not good at all," I say to myself right before I start yelling "Sorry! I'm sorry! Sorry! Excuse me!" as I try to skate as quickly as possible toward an exit, a door, anything to get out and away from the screaming and Wheeler. It's very hard to skate inside, on a slippery floor with my eyes closed, but I'm really trying. I learn I can in fact do it when I practically smash into Lindsey Benson, Mr. Hess' pet. I stop right in front of her, and am staring into her fogged up glasses.

"Oh, hi Lindsey, I didn't see you. You read really well in class, um, how do I get out of here?" This was possibly the weirdest conversation of my life. She points to her left, down a corridor of benches and lockers and a small office, and, at the very end, a door.

"Thanks!" I yell back.

Before I can get to the door, though, a large, squat woman with too tight shorts and a baseball hat steps out of the office and blocks my way. I duck her arm which she's held out like some sort of human stop sign, and head toward the door.

I get momentarily distracted by a particularly loud "Pervert!" screamed right in my ear, and I turn my head to see that not all the girls are freaked out. Some are laughing. Some are snapping towels at me. If it weren't a life or death situation, this just might be the best obstacle course I've ever been on. Then the squat woman is back blowing her whistle like crazy. A bench is blocking my getaway route. Just as I'm slowing to surrender a hand grabs my shirt and yanks me into another room.

"Quick! This way!" It's Jen, and I have been yanked into the showers. She's in nothing but underwear and I don't even want to know who else is there or what they're not wearing.

"Oh no, no, no! Jen?" I absolutely don't want her to think I'm a jerk.

"Just close your eyes and shut up!" She hands me my board and pushes me through the showers, back up past the lockers and back to the door I came in. "Now open your eyes and go!" Jen yells.

I don't ask questions. I'm out the door, in the parking lot, on my board hearing the Hydra's whistle fade as I fly toward home.

At the end of the block I slow, trying to understand what just happened. No time now though; I see Wheeler and his goons coming my way. Now it's my advantage. I may not know the school grounds, but I do know just about every place else in town that's got one, two, three inch steps, curves, tight corners, loose corners, inverts, round poles, which people yell at you if you grind on their property, and which come out to watch.

I decide to go right at them, directly into the middle of the pack. It's the oldest game there is, the game of chicken. Wheeler looks surprised, and before I leave them in a pile, I know that I'm going to win this one. I put my head down and

19

gun it right at his chest. Just as I thought he would, he tries to come at me, changes his mind, looks to Vert for help, then back at me. Vert and Grinder think they're going to jump on me or something. They look to Wheeler because they don't know what to do and have no brains of their own. They've got no signals and I skate through them all as they at the last minute decide they're going to jump me and they end up jumping themselves. Boards are flying, arms are wind-milling and being pulled back painfully, heads banging into each other – It's like something out of the "Three Stooges." I'm smiling big when I pause for a second to watch before I head home, wondering what's for dinner.

While it's fun grinding the usual things like steps and railings and benches, lately I've been trying out other things like milk crates, trash cans, even random pieces of junk like car parts or broken chairs people leave on the curb for trash pickup. I like the unpredictability of it. It's like I have to figure it out every time. I don't get it right every time. Sometimes I end up in a heap, but most of the time I can look at a pile of bricks or a broken picnic table and figure out where I should start the grind, or where to jump it. I've even put some stuff on my route to work so I can practice. Lately I've been working on jumping a roll of carpet someone left on the curb right next to Joe's parking lot – the long way.

I'm just about to try again when I hear "Reynolds!" I of course lose my concentration and wipe out, knocking over Joe's parking lot garbage can and emptying a bag of returnables.

"What the hell are you doing?" In spite of his, what my mom would call, "spicy language," Joe's a nice guy. I think he's older than he looks. He's wiry so his body looks kind of young, but he's got some grey hair and a silver-capped tooth which make him look old. Right now he's wearing a sauce-covered apron and an irritated expression. "And where the hell have you been?" he adds.

"Hi Joe," I answer. If anyone else had ruined a jump, I would be mad, but it's Joe. It's just hard to get mad at Joe.

"You're late!" he yells with his hands on his hips.

"I know, but I told you. New school. Warren Middle. It's further away. Jeez, you're in a good mood. Have another Italian sausage sandwich for lunch? You really should lay off those, Joe. They make you grumpy."

"You know, I run a business here. I got deliveries," Joe yells some more. He can't fool me. I know he's not really that mad. He just needs to let off some steam.

"I'm sorry, Joe. Just tell me where. You know me, I'll get 'em there," I tell him, sort of clicking up my heels like I'm a super pizza delivery kid.

"I can't wait 'til you get your license," Joe grumbles.

"You're going to have to wait a while longer, Joe. I'm only 14."

"You ok?" Now that he's done barking, the nice Joe comes out. He remembers that he saw me take a pretty good spill and he knows too that he probably caused it.

"Huh? Oh, yeah, fine." I check my elbows for blood.

"Good. Wait here." Joe goes inside and I pull out my wristbands. It always takes a second, but I think it through. Red on right, green on left. The headphones don't need any thought. Neither does choosing the music or the volume – up. Joe's back with a couple of pizza boxes in a warmer bag mouthing something at me.

"What?" I only take out one headphone.

"Take those things off!" he screams.

"Dang. Sorry," I say. I know it bothers Joe when I wear both earphones.

"You don't wear those when you're on my clock, right? I don't want you flattened by some bus you don't hear coming."

"I know, I know. I won't." I smile. I think he's said this exact line to me about 500 times.

"Poplar Place. You know where that is, right?"

"'Course."

"I promised they'd be there in a half hour. That was 25 minutes ago," Joe says.

"No problemo. You know me. Ride like the wind."

Joe grins, all done being angry, at least for now. I know he likes me no matter what he says. "You got your wrist things?" he asks.

I raise my fists over my head like I'm Rocky, grab the pizzas, and jump on my board. "I am the champion pizza delivery kid!" I yell.

"And get your butt back right away, you hear? There's going to be more to deliver!" Joe says as he waves at me and heads back inside the restaurant.

CHAPTER FIVE

Carrying pizzas while skating is pretty easy. It's about balance, which is pretty much what skating's about anyway. I get to the corner of Poplar Place and Vine, check my wrist bands, and turn right. I make it in just about exactly five minutes.

After two more deliveries, and more threats from Joe that I'm gonna get hit by a bus if I leave my headphones in, it's beginning to get dark and I'm headed home. I bring home a pizza just about every night I work. I don't mind if my pizza slides, so I carry it under my arm, and I know the buses aren't running as often so I've got both headphones in. I'm taking the long way home because it's nice out – cool and quiet. I like going past the stores on Main when people are slowing down, when the rush of a business day is beginning to end. I coast past the stationary store and spot Tracey Rushing looking at cards inside. She and I went to preschool together about a thousand years ago. I sure didn't know then that she'd look like that now. Maybe I would have paid more attention to her. Little kids don't care about that stuff though. I'm kind of laughing to myself when I see something I didn't see last time I was here.

There's a bunch of kids with boards going into an old warehouse that was closed just last week. I speed up and stop in front of a banner hanging above the door.

"Grand Opening! Westside Freestyle Skate Park" the banner says.

I check my watch to see how much time I got before my mom starts to panic. I go in. Beyond a glass front counter there are kids on skateboards everywhere. A few parents hover around the walls, but mostly it's kids. They're trying to grind, rock, and some try to fakie an ollie. For some kids skateboarding is obviously new. For others, it's clear that this is not their first time on a skateboard. There's a half-pipe in the corner and this kid kick flips down a four stair. There are pipes to grind, ramps everywhere and music blasting out of these huge speakers that hang from the ceiling. This place is awesome.

I didn't even see the guy behind the counter until he says, "Hey. You going in or just gonna stare?" He's kind of short with a long dark ponytail, and an earring. His nametag says "Shido."

"Huh?" I sort of ask. "Yeah. Can I look? Can I go in?"

"Go on in. Check it out. Come back in five minutes or I'm coming after you. You technically gotta have a release form signed before you skate, but I'll let you check it out," he says sort of smiling.

"Thanks."

This place is amazing. It's huge and has tons of stuff like boxes and ramps, bowls, quarter and half pipes. There are even some kids on bikes twisting midair as they race up and over the half pipes. I see a couple of kids on inline skates doing stuff I've never seen kids on inline skates do. And then I notice something: I don't know how I missed it before, but the kid who landed the kick flip down the four stair is Wheeler. Suddenly I'm not so excited.

"Crap!" he yells when he misses landing. I see him looking just to my right and notice that Vert is there too, and then I see Wheeler coming in my direction. I am definitely not interested in any conversation, so I'm outta there.

I ride past Shido who looks at me and says "Well that was fast."

"Yeah, thanks!" I yell as I kick up my board and push the door.

Shido fast walks after me and tries to hand me some paper. "Hey! Take this release to your dad or mom. We let you skate free for the first half hour," he says, jogging now with the paper.

"No thanks. Don't have a dad," I holler as I lose him.

―――――――

Once around the corner, I slow down and think how unfair it is that there's a new skate park in town and before I even get the chance to check it out, to even try it out, Wheeler and his goons are there acting like they own the place.

I'm trying to figure out a way to find out when Wheeler's going so I can go when he's not there just as I open the back door to my house.

"There are some apples in the fridge. Carrots too. Salad if you want, some bananas," my mom calls from the living room when she hears the door shut. She's always trying to get me to eat something besides pizza.

"No thanks, Mom. I brought a pizza home. This is fine," I tell her.

"Chris, you have to eat something from the earth every once in a while. You just can't eat pizza every day," she says as she comes into the kitchen and kisses me on the cheek. She's smiling so I know she's not really angry. She sits down across from me at the table and says, "Well, you have a birthday coming up,"

"Yep, I do. And there is something from the earth in pizza. The sauce is made from tomatoes which I'm pretty sure are things that grow in the ground. And the pepperonis. Aren't they from pepperoni trees?" I say.

"Oh, Chris, cut it out. You know what I mean," she says smiling. "So, what do you want?"

"What do I want?"

"Yes. For your birthday. What would you like? Do you have

any wishes?" She's eating a yogurt, which I will never eat, no matter what.

"Hmm. How 'bout a tattoo?" I roll up the sleeve of my t-shirt to show her where it should go. "Right here."

"Seriously," she fake frowns and points her yogurt spoon at me. "Only if you get 'World's greatest mother' tattooed on your arm."

"My health teacher has a tattoo."

"Try again," she says, scraping out her yogurt container.

"A car would be nice."

"Honey, you're 14. You can't even drive until you're 16."

"I can start taking Driver's Ed when I'm 14 and 9 months," I say. I see her worried look starting so I tell her, "Naw. Just kidding. How 'bout a skateboard? A nice one. Like a Tony Hawk skateboard. Mine's pretty messed up."

She's still got her worried-but-trying-not-to-show-it look. I know it has to do with money. "How much do they cost?"

"About two hundred bucks, I think. You know, cheap," I say, trying to sound sarcastic, like there's no way I'd ever get one and that's ok, but I would love a new board, I really would.

"Oh, Honey. I wish I could, I really do. We're still struggling with some of the debt."

"I know, Mom. I was just kidding. My board's fine. Whatever you decide will be great."

"Of course, you do use it for your job…" she said, looking like she's doing some math in her head.

"Yeah, I do, so you could say I need it for work. And I haven't killed myself yet…" I say this without thinking which is how a lot of stupid things come out of my mouth.

I see her look sharp at me like she just burned herself on something.

"Sorry, Mom. Bad joke. I didn't mean it that way."

"I know," she says quickly shaking it off. "Maybe we can find a used one. Do kids do that? Would that work?"

"Sure, Mom. Anything at all is great." I'm trying to change the subject because I hate making my mom upset. "Joe wants me to get my license so I can drive the pizzas instead of skate them around town, but I kind of like being a pizza delivery kid who skateboards instead of drives."

"14 and nine months you said?" Mom asks.

"Yep. I hit that mark two months ago," I say.

"It's hard to believe, but you're right. You're going to be 15 before I know it," and then she looks sort of sad again as she messes up my hair and stands up to put her yogurt container in the sink.

CHAPTER SIX

I'm not sure why, maybe it's boredom, but later that same week I'm sitting in my room, just kind of looking around for something to do and I see the corner of my English book sticking out from under my dresser. I pull it out, blow off a couple of dust bunnies and give another try: "Even the dravest... Br...bravest...that are slave..." Concentrate you idiot. "... slain...Shall not bis...dis...dissemble...Their surprise...On walking to find...Bal...val...or. Screw this!" It's useless. I just suck at reading and that's all there is to it. I chuck the book at the closed door and hear my mom breathing on the other side.

"Chris?" she asks. I didn't hear her come up the stairs.

"Yeah," I say casual-like. I don't want her asking me a bunch of questions, I really don't. I can't guarantee that I'm going to be real polite.

"Can I come in?"

"Suppose so. It's your house," I tell her. She starts to open the door slowly, but the book gets wedged under it and the door stops.

"Wait. I got it," I say. Already I feel bad about being rude.

"It's our house, by the way," she says stepping in and looking around at my messy room. I can tell that she wants to say something about it, but she doesn't.

"Your house, our house. Whatever." Looks like I just can't help it. Rude is just where I'm at today.

"Just wondering how school is going."

I can't lie, but I don't want to get her all upset either. I settle for frowning and shrugging. "School's school. How do you suppose it went? How did your school go?" I say. I don't know if I want to change the subject really. I kind of want to talk about school and how much I hate it, well some of it, and I kind of don't want to tell her anything about anything.

"Great, actually. The kids were really funny today. They told me all about what they did over the weekend. This one kid, he's super cute – his name is Oliver, he told me he went to see the Grand Canyon and then I said 'Really! The Grand Canyon! That sounds so exciting!' and then he said 'No, no, not the Grand Canyon. I went to see my grandfather! It wasn't that exciting.' Oh I tried so hard not to laugh," she says. She really does love teaching those kids. And I know she's really good at it too.

"Can I go back?" I say quietly. I don't want to spoil the moment or her good mood or whatever, but I figure it's worth a shot. "To Kennedy? Please?"

"Go back?"

"Yeah. You know, go back to Kennedy. It's not too late, is it?" I say trying to sound nonchalant.

"Oh, Chris," she sighs, sitting down on the bed. I'm mad at myself for not keeping my mouth shut. "Kennedy's not the place for you. They didn't challenge you there…"

"Well, they didn't make me feel like a complete idiot either," I say, getting mad.

"Honey, I know it's tough, but it's going to get better. You haven't even met -"

"What happens when you get new kids in your class? Didn't you say once that you got new kids all the time?" I say, cutting her off.

"Well, not all the time. But it's different for little kids. For one thing, my students are with me all day long. They're little, Chris. They're mostly just really sweet –"

"Exactly my point," I say, cutting her off again.

"Huh?" she asks. "Look, just because they're little doesn't mean they don't have a hard time sometimes. It's just different.

It isn't easy for a lot of them. It isn't easy for me either. Some kids come from some pretty lousy home situations and they bring all that to school. They haven't learned to hide it yet. They have so few skills to deal with their situations," she explains. "They still deal with all of that whether they're new to the school or not."

"And our home life is peachy? Normal?" I hated that I couldn't shut up when I knew I really should.

"Chris, you know we can't change the past," she says getting quiet and looking down at her hands.

Rather than say anything else, I get up to leave. I watch my mom sigh again and hang her head. I can't help it. I tell her, "You don't think the past has anything to do with the present?"

"No, I don't. At least – Chris," she's talking to me real intense-like, like if she could she would drill the words into my thick skull: "Chris, you were born with this, with dyslexia. You can't help it. You were also born smart. And because you're smart, you can deal with it, I know it. A lot of people have."

I stare right back at her which is not easy to do. My mom has a death stare when she wants to. My plan to leave the room is no good. I can't escape the death stare.

"It has nothing to do with your father!" she says.

I nod, slowly.

"I spoke with the school today, Chris. Everyone admits that your transition to Warren hasn't been ideal. We all agree on that. It's taken some time to get all the paperwork worked out, but the principal assured me that tomorrow you'll meet with your Special Ed counselor. I've spoken with her on the phone. Her name is Ms. James. She seems very nice."

"Ok. Fine," I say. It's no use. I just can't defend myself from my mother's stare. I decide now's a good time to brush my teeth. I go past her to the bathroom.

"Go brush your teeth, Chris. It will all work out, you'll see. See you in the morning," she says and gives me a quick hug.

I go to the bathroom feeling like I just lost a battle.

The next morning I find myself being bumped and pushed in the hallways of Warren Middle while I try to find a room I haven't been to before. Again I got this little piece of paper with a room number on it, and again I'm trying not to look like an idiot by walking into the wrong room. I finally walk into what I really hope is the Resource Room and at first I don't see anyone.

"Just a minute, I'll be right with you," a lady's voice says from behind a half-closed door. It's not a normal classroom I notice. There are tables and chairs instead of desks and there's even a couple of big easy chairs. There's a book shelf, a rug, some huge pillows on the floor and a boom box on the window ledge.

"Well, hello!" the same voice says. I turn around and my mouth drops open. Great. Just great. It's the lady whose lunch I spilled all over her.

"Oh…It's you," she says. I panic for a second before she adds "You're not here to throw food on me again, are you?"

"Uh. No, no I'm not. Sorry about that…" I say. She doesn't seem mad because she's smiling, but I might be wrong. I start to move toward the door.

"Where are you going?" she asks me, her hands going to her hips.

I stop, but I don't turn around. "I don't think this is the right room. I don't think this is gonna work out," I mumble.

"You're Chris Reynolds, right? Well it better work out, because meeting you is on my to-do list for the day and I always like to finish my to-do list before I go home," she tells me. She's not swearing like Joe usually does, but something about her reminds me of Joe.

I turn around. "To-do list? I'm on your to-do list? I'm not sure I understand," I say, waiting.

"It turns out you don't really get to decide whether or not to stay. You have to stay because I have to sit and talk with you because you, Chris Reynolds are on my list of people I have to talk to today before I go home. Does that make more sense?" she says, pulling out a chair at a table for me to sit.

"I guess so," I say.

"Have a seat. I don't bite, and my clothes are all wash and wear, so the mess you dumped on me the other day? It's like it never happened." She smiles and then says "Cool shirt. I know that place. I like the pizza."

"Huh?" I say. I have no idea what she's talking about.

"Pizza. Joe's has good pizza," she says pointing at my shirt. "I like the veggie the best. Actually, lately I've been getting the calzone. When I go, that is. I'd eat there more often, but I don't need the calories. Not a problem that you have, probably. What's your favorite?"

"What?" I say. I don't know if I've ever just had a normal conversation with a teacher or anyone like a teacher, so her friendliness kind of throws me.

"Pizza. What's your favorite topping?" she asks me again.

"Oh. I like them all I guess. Except for maybe…"

"Except for which?"

"Except, uh, the veggie. I'm not a big vegetable eater," I say, smiling.

She's smiling back and says "You don't have to be at your age. Although you should. 'Course the tomato sauce is pretty good for you. There are tomatoes in the tomato sauce. That's a vegetable – or is it a fruit? I never know which," she says. "Anyways, there are all kinds of studies that say tomatoes have all kinds of great health benefits. Antioxidants, stuff like that."

"Oh yeah? I was just trying to convince my mom about the 'there are vegetables in pizza sauce' thing," I tell her.

"Did she buy it?" she asks. And then suddenly she says, "Oh! I'm sorry! I know your name and I haven't even told you mine. My name is Ms. James. I'm your Special Services Provider. Actually that sounds really lame. Let's just say I'm here to help you. I'm here to help you with whatever you need help with – homework, adjusting to a new school, family stuff," she says. I stand and shake her hand, then she picks up a manila envelope that I see has my name on the front. I think I know what's in the envelope: proof from my old school that I can't read, that I'm basically a middle school idiot and I sit back down.

"Oh my, a young man with manners. Shaking hands when being introduced and standing no less. A rare commodity these days. I'd certainly like to meet your parents," Ms. James says smiling.

"Parent," I tell her.

"I'm sorry?" she says.

"I said 'parent' not 'parents.' I don't have a dad. Well, I did, but he's dead. Um," I say. I've never found a way to say this that doesn't sound weird.

"Oh, yes. I remember now," she mumbles, quickly pulling the papers out of the envelope and reading through them. "Right. It's just you and your mom." She looks at me again smiling. "So I see you've transferred here from, Kennedy Middle School, isn't that right?"

"From Kennedy, yeah. I was at Kennedy from first through seventh," I tell her. I don't want to make her feel bad about forgetting the deal about my dad. It's not her fault that it's so awkward to talk about.

"Well, anyway. Wherever you came from, Chris, you're here now," she says. "In this classroom you can call me 'Cora.' In the hallway, or anywhere else in the school, call me 'Ms. James'. Protocol you know, but here, 'Cora' will work just fine."

I nod and she looks at the papers again. "How long have you known you have dyslexia?"

"You mean officially?" I'm a little relieved to get the word 'dyslexia' out of the way. I was dreading going through all that testing again.

"Yes, officially."

"Since last fall," I tell her.

"I assume that's when you were tested," she says scribbling something down on the paper.

"Right."

"And you were never tested before that?"

"Nope," I say. I'm not sure why she's asking me all this if she's got it all on the papers.

"Why not?" she asks. She stops writing and looks at me.

"Why wasn't I tested before? Well, I guess because I was doing ok in school and stuff."

"Aha. Yes, I see you get pretty good grades," she says shuffling through the papers again.

"I'm a good memorizer."

"I have no doubt of that. Your mom is a teacher, right?" I know she knows this too because it's written on the paper somewhere. I'm not sure why she's asking me this stuff if she already knows the answers. I'm thinking this is going to be a whole lot of boring.

"Yep, Mom's a teacher," I say.

"Until it caught up with you," she adds. Now she's looking

right at me.

"Huh? Until what caught up with me? Look, I don't want to get in any trouble for something that happened at my old school," I tell her. "To tell you the truth, I don't even want to be here. Not here in this room and not here at Warren," I tell her.

"I don't want to be here either," she says. She's not looking at the papers any more. She tosses them on the table and just sits there for a minute looking at me. And then she says "I'd rather be on a tropical island somewhere sipping an icy, cold drink," she says, taking a second to lean back and sigh. "But this is my second choice, so here I am," she says, no longer daydreaming about Tahiti.

I have no idea what to say, so I just sort of stare at her quickly then at the table.

She pulls out a booklet from the envelope and says "Ok. Let's get down to business. I have a test for you to take."

"I told you. I took one last fall," I tell her. I'm starting to get mad again.

"This is another one," she says. She sees that I'm not making any move to pick up the booklet "Look, humor me. In my business, we give a lot of tests. It's just part of the deal. Besides, some of them actually help," she says, quieter now. "You wouldn't rather be in Hess' class, would you?" she asks.

"This will get me out of English?" I figure I might as well play this as best I can.

"English class goes until 10 of, right?" she says looking at the clock above the door.

"Yeah, I think so," I say.

"Oh, I think you can afford to miss an English class," she says, smiling.

"Ok by me," I say and I take the test booklet and grab a pencil.

CHAPTER SEVEN

About a week later I'm coming down the hallway, doing my best to ignore everyone, when I see it: "Retard" in huge, black letters on the front of my locker. My skateboard's inside, so there's no pretending the locker isn't mine. I open it as fast as I can, grab my board, and slam the locker door so hard it bounces. I slam it again, it latches, and I take off. I'm so mad I can hardly see straight. I so want to jump on my skateboard and scream down the hallways, but I hold it all in until I reach the double doors. I slam them open, and throw my board so hard down the steps I think it might break. I'm so pissed I don't even care. I run to catch up with the board and fly home, letting the tears run sideways across my cheeks.

———

Later that same week a storm looks like it's headed our way just as school lets out. Skating in the rain, even a little rain, is not a good idea. It can ruin your bearings making the ride rough and slower. I'm not ready to buy a new deck or bearings if mine get waterlogged. I don't have the money, so I'm looking up at the clouds gauging how far off the rain is. I'm just past the school steps, looking at the dark clouds when Jen almost skates right into me.

"Oh! Sorry, I didn't see you!" I say, jumping off my board.

"No, I'm sorry. I didn't mean to surprise you," Jen says, laughing.

"Oh, no…no. I mean, yes, you did, but…" Between the coming rain and seeing Jen on a skateboard, I have no idea which is more distracting.

"Something wrong?" Jen asks me.

"No! I mean, no. I'm just checking out the weather, and…"

She's looking at me like I've got something stuck to my face or something.

"I guess I never thought of you as a skateboarder," I tell her.

"Oh! Yeah. Since I was a little kid. My dad insisted I take all kinds of lessons when I was a kid. It was his idea to get me involved in something wherever we lived. Of course my dad had visions of me becoming another Shawn Johnson. Gold medal and all that," Jen says, kicking her board up and showing me the underside as she spins a back wheel with her hand.

"Yeah, I get it," I tell her. She does have a pretty nice board – it's a Baker deck with Thunder trucks and Bones bearings and wheels.

"You're pretty good," she says, dropping her board back to the ground.

"Thanks. Better than at reading poetry I guess," I shrug.

It's really nice when she smiles, which she does now. "Don't worry about that. Poetry isn't everything. Skate with me?"

"Uh." A roll of thunder comes on cue. I look up and say "You sure?"

Jen takes off and I follow. Now is not the time to stop skating just because of a little rain. She's surprisingly good. She's not doing tricks really, but she can take curves easy and really weaves without any effort. I show her an ollie and then a pop shuv-it. When I kick flip, she laughs and claps. I laugh too, knowing that she knows that I'm showing off.

"Why don't you try it?" I ask her.

"No way! My lessons only covered staying on the board and weaving. Ollies and pop shuv-its and kick flips were for the kids in the advanced class," she laughs, racing ahead of me.

"I could show you," I yell after her.

Just as I say that, the sprinkling rain turns to for real rain and

I look at Jen kind of worried. Jen grabs my hand and I have no choice but to ignore the rain and what it might do to my bearings. Right now, I couldn't care less. We skate side-by-side until we get to the corner where I have to turn left to go to work and she has to go right to go home.

"That was really fun. See you later?" Jen lets go of my hand, and flashes another fantastic smile.

"Yeah. Great. Sure. I mean, that would be great, uh, when?" I say. I know I sound like an idiot, but I want her to know for sure that I would be more than ok with doing this again – rain or no rain.

"Oh, whenever. I usually have my board with me too, like you. Maybe tomorrow after school?"

"I might have to work, I mean, yeah. That sounds great. Sure. Tomorrow then?" Joe can fire me if he wants. I don't care. If I'm late to work because I was skating with Jen, well, then, I guess I'm fired.

"Ok. See you tomorrow!" Jen calls as she skates toward home.

"Yeah! See you!" I'm drenched, I hope I wasn't out long enough to ruin my board. I roll into the kitchen of Joe's, looking for a towel. I nearly run into Jorge and Sally who are putting together pizza boxes.

"Hola, Jorge! Hiya Sally!" I yell.

"Hay lluvia!" calls Jorge, "You are all wet!"

"Si!" I say looking down at my wet clothes, smiling.

"It's really raining out there huh?" asks Sally.

"Yep! Raining like crazy." I nod, grab a towel, and start to dry off my board first and then my hair and shoulders. I notice a monkey bobble-head on the shelf behind the towels and wonder where it came from. I don't remember ever seeing it before.

"Where the hell have you been?" Joe yells.

I try to pretend like I've been there for hours just flicking the bobble-head. "Huh? Say what?" I turn and look at him, still flicking the bobble-head.

"Oh, Jeez! You're wet. How did you get so wet? Don't you know enough to come in out of the rain? You know you shouldn't skate in the rain. Look, there's a spare chef's uniform in the utility closet. You work the front. Sally's doing the deliveries," Joe complains and then stomps off to the back.

"I'm not old enough to work the front," I yell to the back.

"You ain't old enough to drive either, and it's wet out there. You don't want to ruin your board. Just don't pour any beer," Joe yells back as he heads back out to the front. "And put your board away!" He stops again and looks at me real close. "What you need is a girlfriend to make you be on time."

"A girlfriend? That's a good idea, Joe. Maybe my mom will take me to the mall to get one," I tell him, grinning from ear to ear.

———————

I'm wearing the chef's coat and the too-big black and white checkered pants wiping the counter for the millionth time when I notice that it's 9:00. Time has never moved so fast at work. It feels like it was just a second ago that Jen and I were skating down the middle of the street together. I've relived that moment about a million times since it happened.

"Nice job tonight, kid. For your first night on the floor, that is," Joe tells me, pulling off his apron and reaching out to take mine.

"Yeah, thanks, if I don't mind giving up sleep and homework." I nod toward the clock to let Joe know. Suddenly it dawns on me how late it is and how much homework I have to do when I get home.

"Oh yeah, right. Sorry. Later than I thought," Joe says looking a little worried.

"Can I go now?" I ask him.

"Yeah. I mean, no. I gotta deal with the order of tomatoes that came in today with Jorge in the kitchen. Could you do one more thing? Could you go up to the Crow's Nest and bring down some coffee? If I gotta stay up to do this, I need coffee. Some real coffee, not the stuff here. It's in my freezer, in the door. Here are the keys," Joe says, tossing me the big ring of keys he takes out of his pocket.

"Crow's Nest? What's the Crow's Nest?" I ask him. I have never heard of this before.

"My apartment. You know, where I live?" He sees me staring at him. "You didn't know I lived above the restaurant? It's up those stairs in the back. It's not much, but its home to me," Joe says, nodding toward the top of the stairs.

"Yeah, sure. I'll get the coffee," I shrug and head toward the stairs.

There's a bunch of keys on the ring, so it takes me a minute to find the right one. Finally, I find the one that opens the door, and I step inside. The one light that's on by the door shows that the room I step into is full of skateboard stuff – posters, old boards – some broken clean in half – ribbons, trophies, a bunch of issues of *Thrasher*, random wheels on a coffee table, different size trucks on a table in the little kitchen, and photos, lots of photos. I stop to look at one on the fridge. It's Joe, but younger. He's wearing a medal around his neck and he's holding his board above his head, looking like he's yelling something. I stare at it and all the skateboard stuff for a while, circling back into the living room and looking more closely at the ribbons and a couple of trophies on top of the TV. "Dang," I whisper to myself. "Joe was no joke." I wonder how long ago this was, so I start looking for dates, years on the trophies or ribbons and find a few that say 1999, and then a few more that say 2000 and 2001. "That's about 15 years ago," I say to myself again. I wonder why I never knew this about Joe, why he's never said anything about winning all this, about being a competitive skater.

"Hey, what happened? You fall asleep up there?" I hear Joe yell from downstairs.

"Sorry! I'm coming. Be there in a minute!" I yell back and head back to the fridge. I open the freezer door slowly, trying to understand all of what I'm seeing. I find a bag of coffee beans in the door and head back out. Just before I turn the knob I see a gold and silver board leaning against the wall. It's not broken. In fact, it looks to be the least used of them all. The least used and maybe the sweetest. I bend down to pick it up, but I change my mind, and turn the knob to leave. On the other side of the door, I check that it's locked and head back down the stairs.

"Jeez! I thought maybe you'd decided to clean my bathroom," Joe says as I hand him the coffee, and he heads back into the kitchen to Jorge and the tomatoes.

"I'm taking off. Good night, Joe," I tell him, not ready to ask him anything yet. I'm going to need a minute to try to figure this out on my own.

"See ya," Joe says, already busy sorting the tomatoes.

CHAPTER EIGHT

The next day in school, Ms. James becomes my new best friend. "You're with me today," she whispers to me as she signals to Mr. Hess that I'll be with her instead of him in English. Mr. Hess looks none too pleased, and it all happens so fast Wheeler misses his chance to make a smart aleck comment. I grab my backpack and walk out.

I'm as happy as a clam until I see Vert turn the corner. He's late to class, so he's in a hurry, but not in such a hurry that he forgets: "Going to the Retard room, Reynolds? Have a good time!"

"Excuse me!" Ms. James blocks his way.

"Excuse me, Ms. James. Pardon me, but I'm late to class, I really hate to be late," Vert says and walks around her and into the classroom.

Ms. James is really mad, I can tell, but I tell her, "It's ok, Ms. James. He's kind of an idiot, but it's fine. Really."

"It's not ok, and it's definitely not fine," Ms. James says. "What is his name? Charles Something, is that it?" She squints, trying to come up with his last name.

"Ms. James, really. It doesn't bother me. Let's just go. Please," I ask.

"It bothers me, Chris. It bothers me a lot. If no one corrects that kid or anyone who uses those words on people, nothing's going to get better. Those kinds of people are going to think that it's ok, that there's nothing wrong with it," Ms. James says, getting louder.

"Ok. You're right. It's not ok. It's wrong. In fact it's really wrong. It's also wrong to waste time out here in the hallway isn't it?" I say, trying to get Ms. James to head to her room.

"If only he knew just how smart you are," Ms. James says. "It is wrong to waste time on people like that. Come on. Let's get going. I'll talk to Principal Pearlman after school today, see if she can help me figure out that kid's name."

We head down the hall and watch a couple of other kids run late into classrooms, doing their best not to fall as they round the corners.

We get to Ms. James' room and she asks me to take a seat. I check out the diplomas on the wall and wonder about the people in the photos on her desk as she shuffles papers.

"What's this?" I ask. There's a framed piece of paper that was obviously written by a kid. It's in dark purple and it says 'Make new frienbs, but keeg the olb. One is zilver and the other is pold.'

"Oh, my son did that when he was in third grade. It's supposed to say 'Make new friends, but keep the old. One is silver and the other is gold,'" Ms. James says as she looks up from her papers.

"He was like me, then," I say.

She nods. "Yep, he was like you. I got your test results back," Ms. James says, pulling one sheet from a stack and sitting down across from me at the table. She doesn't say anything else about the test or her son or anything. She just looks at me.

"So? Wait. I know. I'm dyslexic. I reverse letters. I can't read. I can't spell. I know that. You know that. So what else is new?" I say, wondering why she's not telling me this herself.

"Well, at least I have a handle on some of the specifics," she says after she takes a deep breath, "and by the way, you don't have all your information straight."

"Huh? What information? I'm not dyslexic?" I ask.

"No, I didn't say you didn't have dyslexia. You do. That's pretty certain. What you don't have right is that dyslexia isn't always just about reversing letters. And it's not a matter of you not being able to read or spell, but more about your difficulty in using and processing not just words, but maybe numbers too. It's like this," Ms. James says, looking like she's really concentrating, like she really wants me to get it. "You have a language-based disability in using and processing or understanding not just written language, but spoken language too and with numbers. Have you ever noticed any difficulty understanding numbers?" she asks me.

"I'm ok at math, actually, but I kind of don't get the whole quantity thing in science class. We're doing this right now in science actually. Like when they talk about how when you pour a liquid from one kind of container into another, it is the same amount even though it doesn't look like it? I don't get that at all," I tell her. "It's weird that the two things could be related. And that whole thing about not understanding spoken language is true sometimes too. That can get really bad when I'm nervous or mad – like when other kids start messing with me," I say, quieter. I sit there for a minute thinking about this, about how when Wheeler says stuff to me, I just sit there trying to understand what he's saying – light years away from coming up with a good comeback.

"Hello? Chris? Is this making sense to you?" Ms. James asks. She's waving her hand in front of my face to get my attention.

"Oh, sorry. Uh, yeah, that makes sense," I say. "So now what?"

"Well, we'll take a longer look at what type of dyslexia you have. We'll look for some specific manifestations. Possible courses of treatment. That sort of thing," she says, looking at the paper. "There's a program called the Orton-Gillingham method that's had a lot of success with kids like you," she says, looking at me.

This is not something I've heard before. I usually just hear "You have dyslexia." I didn't know there were different kinds. I'm trying to get a look at my scores, but she's holding the paper so I can't see it.

"This says you get your letters confused by mixing up your b's with your d's. You reverse them. With my son we called that a Monkey Flip," she says and then smiles. "But you also skip over letters or rely solely on what a word sounds like when you write, and sometimes the same word sounds different to you so you come up with another spelling for the same word. Sound familiar?"

"Is that supposed to be funny?" I ask her. It feels pretty strange to hear her say exactly what I have never been able to say. She does it so easily, I'm kind of mad. Besides, I've been called lots of things – "Stupid," "Dumbo," "Retard," "Moron," but I've never been called a "Monkey," and never by a teacher. Suddenly I'm not interested in my test results. "Whatever, I mean yes, it all sounds familiar, but I'm not a monkey," I tell her and slouch.

"I wasn't calling you a monkey. That's how my son described what the letters did when he was reading. Well, anyhow, understanding it as `Monkey Flipping' helped Jimmy when he was in third grade," Ms. James says.

"I'm not in third grade," I say, calming down some.

"I'm quite aware of that," she says, looking right at me again.

"So, what else did the test results say?" I ask.

"Other people may think you're slow or lazy even. Actually, I know – and I suspect you know – that you're rather smart. Gifted even," she says. She's not smiling or laughing. She's not making fun of me. She's serious.

"I saw your locker. I saw what someone wrote. The janitor

will have it gone by tomorrow. Any idea who did it? Was it that Charles kid, the one we ran into outside of Hess' class?" she asks me, real stern.

I shake my head and shrug. Even if I did know, I wasn't about to tell.

"You know, Chris, just because a person has difficulty reading doesn't mean they're stupid. You know this, right? And kids can be pretty cruel to one another when they feel threatened or when they meet someone else who's even just a little different from them. You know this too, right? Albert Einstein was dyslexic," she says. She's getting real intense now, leaning closer. "So was Leonardo da Vinci, Pablo Picasso, John F. Kennedy, George Washington, Thomas Jefferson, Thomas Edison, Jennifer Aniston, Jay Leno, Tom Cruise -"

"W.B. Yeats. I know the list. Remember: We dyslexics aren't stupid," I tell her, but I'm beginning to think that she's not all that bad.

"W.B. Yeats? The poet? I thought English was your weakness," she says, smiling.

"Reading out loud in front of people is a weakness for sure. I actually like a lot of poets. My dad taught it. English, I mean," I tell her.

"Oh. I guess that's kind of ironic isn't it?" she says.

"Kinda," I shrug and smile.

"Well. Ok. Well, you're going to have to bear with me a moment because I've got to give you the spiel, right?"

"Spiel on. It's better than sitting in Hess' class," I tell her.

Ms. James takes a deep breath and smiles. "As you probably know, dyslexia can manifest itself in many ways, not all of them negative. Some dyslexics become world leaders, some inventors, some musicians, some athletes. For example –"

"Magic Johnson is another one," I say.

"Yes. The basketball player. I just learned about him. I'm not surprised you know about him," she says. "Now, I have to do a bit of history here, so please bear with me a little longer. Your father died when you were five, is that right?"

"Five. Right. It was a long time ago," I say, looking down at my hands.

"That must have been really hard," she says quiet, looking at me.

I shrug and tell her, "Can we talk about dyslexia?"

"Sure thing," she says. "Dyslexia and all the famous people who have it. Who knows? You might be on this list someday."

I smile and laugh, "Yeah, right."

———

It's funny how I never get tired of pizza even though I work at a pizza place and I eat pizza just about every day. I'm thinking this while I'm once again sitting by myself in the cafeteria the next week eating leftover pizza for lunch.

"Hi," I hear Jen say.

I look up and see Jen smiling. "Hey," I say back.

"Expecting anybody?" she asks.

"Nope." Just me and my cold pizza enjoying each other's company.

"Can I sit here?" she asks me, as if she has to.

"Sure," I say and motion with my hand holding the pizza, "Have a seat."

"I see you've dried off," Jen says, looking I think at my hair.

For a split second I'm confused and then I remember, "Oh, yeah," I say. "You too? Did you get soaked?"

"Totally soaked. My mom accused me of falling in a river. I had to peel everything off I was so drenched when I got home."

"My boss at work let me have it when I got there. I had to change into some old, leftover chef's clothes," I tell her, laughing.

"Oh that's right, you had to go to work soaked. How hilarious! Oh man! That was fun, wasn't it?" she asks.

"That was awesome. I've never skated with anybody like that before," I say. I've forgotten about eating pizza.

"Yeah it really was a lot of fun," Jen agrees. A couple of really long awkward seconds go by and then Jen asks "Mind if I ask you something?"

"Um, ok. Depends on what it is," I say. She looks serious so I'm not sure I want to hear her question.

"Ok. I'll ask, but you don't have to answer, all right?" she says.

"Um, ok," I say. This does not sound like it's going to be a good question.

"Why did you transfer here, and does that have something to do with Ms. James pulling you out of class?"

"Because, and yes," I answer. I definitely don't want to be a jerk, but I don't want to set myself up to be called a moron either.

"Well, I guess that's a better answer than none," she says and gets up to leave.

I regret sounding like a jerk. The last thing I want to do is get rid of her, so I tell her "I'm sorry. I'm just distracted or something. I don't mean to sound like a jerk. The reason why my mom had me transfer here is that, well, I'm dyslexic and my old school didn't have any services for me," I say looking around to see if anyone is eavesdropping.

"Aha. I knew it was something," she says and sits back down. "You know, you can talk to me. I just want to be your friend. I sort of know what dyslexia is, I think," she says and then waves her hand in front of her face. "Anyways. I don't care about that stuff. I just had fun with you the other day. That was really great. We agreed to go skateboarding again remember? Maybe I could actually learn something besides staying on my board and going around curves," she says and laughs.

"Uh, sure. I'll teach you whatever tricks you want. Uh, how do you know about dyslexia?" I ask.

"I wrote a report about it last year. It's a reading thing, right? Something about reversing letter or mixing up letters or something?"

"Yeah, it's something like that," I tell her.

"So? Is that so bad? Is that a crime?" she says smiling again.

"Bad? No, it's not 'bad,' and it's definitely not a crime. It can make it hard to read and almost impossible to read in front of people, as you saw," I say, explaining a little.

"Yeah, well, that does suck, for sure. But who cares? I think you're nice and fun and funny – dyslexia and all," she tells me. "Besides. Everybody's got problems, you know? Don't think you're so special," she says, kind of joking, glaring at me.

"Oh, I do not think I'm so special, that's for sure," I laugh.

"Well, I do. I do think you're special. In a good way," she says and grabs her trays and leaves.

I think she means that she likes me, but I'm still a little mystified. I remember my pizza and finish it off, not tasting a bit of it.

CHAPTER NINE

The next week, as I skate through the back door of Joe's Pizza, I see Joe helping Jorge out with spinning the dough. I flick the bobble-head, and kick my board up.

"My God, you made it on time!" Joe says, looking away from the flying dough.

"Yep. No distractions today," I tell him.

"Well, it looks like it's gonna be slow, so I might have some cleaning up for you to do."

"Ok, boss," I say, still playing with the bobble-head.

"Jorge, how are the mushrooms from the new provider? Are they ok? Did they look good and fresh and crunchy when they came in?" Joe asks Jorge.

"Yes, crunchy. Very fresh. And clean, too," Jorge says. I don't know why Joe insists on showing Jorge how to make the dough. Looks to me like Jorge is way better at it than Joe.

While Joe and Jorge discuss the goodness of mushrooms, I'm thinking about how I want to ask Joe something. I give it a go. "Hey, Joe. Got a question."

"Fire away," Joe says as he leaves Jorge to the dough and heads to the front of the store.

"When I was up in your apartment – the Crow's Nest – I saw a bunch of skateboarding stuff. I didn't know you were a skateboarder." It seems weird to be nervous to talk to Joe about anything, but I can't figure out why he never told me that he skated when he knows that I skate. It's like he's hiding something or something.

Joe's busy pushing in chairs and arranging red pepper flake shakers. "Yeah, a little. For a while. Previous lifetime though," he says without stopping.

"How long did you skate?" I ask, watching him.

"Seventeen years," he says like it's no big deal.

"Seventeen years?" I yell.

"Started when I was seven. Quit when I was twenty-four." Joe moves on to picking invisible crumbs off the tables.

"What? Dude! Seventeen years is a long time! Why did you quit?" I wish he'd stop messing with the tables and look at me.

"Got my bell rung too many times. Besides. It was time. Twenty-four year old legs aren't the same as fourteen year old legs," he says. He stops moving around and is looking at me, but he doesn't seem proud or braggy. He looks serious-like.

"I saw a silver and gold skateboard up there."

"Yep. That's old quicksilver. Back in my day I was a would-be contender," he says and smiles. "That board was the best back then." And then he's back arranging salt and pepper shakers.

"What happened?"

"To the board? Nothing. It's still good. Not as good as the boards out today, but it's still a good board," he says.

"No, not with the board, with you. What happened? You said you got your bell rung. Did you hit your head real bad?" I ask.

Joe lets out a long breath. "I was doing an air trick and came down on my noggin' and sustained a brain injury. You're marking up my floor," he says and he points down to my board which I had absent mindedly dropped down and stood on, rolling while I listened.

I can tell he doesn't want to talk about what happened. I look at him a second and then say, "Joe, this floor can't get any worse than it already is." I wait a second then ask, "So you quit?"

"Well, after I got out of the hospital, I hung up my board for good, doctor's orders," Joe says quickly, and then, right on time, the phone rings and Joe runs to the back to answer it, "Hello, Joe's Pizza. Free delivery. The special today is large pepperoni, $12.99."

I stand there a few seconds longer picturing the bad fall, then shrug and get busy because Joe has stuck his head around the door and is waving his hand at me which means 'Quit standing there and do something!' There are a couple of orders ready to go out, so pick up the boxes and head out, making sure I got my wristbands.

———

On my way I think about Joe and wonder what he was trying to do when he wiped out so bad. What does he mean by an air trick, I wonder. I imagine it's some kind of high jump, but there are a lot of those. Then I imagine myself making some amazing jumps while not letting the pizza even slide inside the box, but I wait for the real jumps until I'm coming back with empty bags. After I deliver two pizzas just a block apart, I head back. Clearing the garbage cans lined up along the side of Joe's is my latest challenge. I have to get up some good speed, but after just a couple of fails, I can usually clear them easily.

"Hey, Jorge. Thanks for loading up Mrs. Perowitz's order with all those black olives," I say before I'm all the way back in the kitchen. "She gave me a big tip. Here's your cut," I leave Jorge $5 on the back counter.

"Thanks, man," Jorge says, taking a break from flinging dough.

"De nada. Hey Joe! I'm gone. Gotta get home," I yell. I don't see Joe, but I know he's in the front, cleaning tables, or sweeping or taking an order. "See you tomorrow!"

"What do you mean you're gone? It's Friday," Joe yells then appears in the back carrying the broom and dust pan.

"I'm tired. Been a tough week," I tell him. "Besides. It's not so busy tonight. Can I go home, pleeease? Pretty pleeease? I'll be here 15 minutes early tomorrow to help you prep. Deal?" I ask, trying my best to look like a sad puppy.

"I'm not so sure you'll want to leave, Chris," Joe says, nod toward the dining room. "You just might want to rethink leaving."

"What? What are you talking about," I ask. Joe's got this stupid grin on his face that I can't figure out.

"Someone's waiting for you, Dude," he says, leaning closer. "It might be the reason why you were on time today," then he motions toward the dining room with his head again. "In there, sitting by the front windows."

I look around the corner into the dining room and see Jen sitting alone at a table, sipping a soda and reading a textbook. I stare back at Joe. "Why is she here? I mean, she's here?"

"Get your butt in there, Buddy, before you catch any flies!" Joe laughs, closes my mouth, and opens the door to the dining room wider.

"Huh?" I say.

"She's here to see you, Bobble-head. She asked if you were working. Go on!" Joe practically pushes me through the door.

"Hi," I say as I jog a little to keep from falling, thanks to Joe's shove.

"Hi! Ready?" Jen says, and rolls her board out from under the table.

"Did you come here by yourself? You know, this isn't a very safe part of town," I tell her. It's weird to see Jen at Joe's.

She shrugs and tells me, "I figure you'd skate me home."

I'm trying not to turn red again, trying to think fast here. "How long have you been here?" I ask, trying my best to act like it's no big deal that she's come to Joe's to go skateboarding with me.

"'Bout half an hour. Got my homework for Monday done."

"But how d-d-d-did you?" I have never stuttered before, but suddenly I seem to have developed a stutter.

"How did I find out where Joe's Pizza is? Everybody knows where Joe's is. Anyway, Ms. James told me you worked most days after school. We're actually pretty close. She's my advisor," Jen says as she puts her papers and books in her backpack. "She's neat. You'll like her. She wouldn't tell me everything, though. Student confidentiality and all that."

"'Everything'? What 'everything'? What else did you ask her?" I don't want to sound rude, but I am really curious.

"Nothing really. Not any scandalous information," Jen says putting quotation marks in the air and making her eyes go big. "Just curious. Trying to find out more about you. That's not a crime is it?" Jen asks.

"No, it's not, but..." I'm having a hard time taking this information in. "Uh, no. It's not a crime," I say lamely.

"Why do you wear a green wristband on one wrist and a red one on the other?" Jen asks, pointing to my wrists. "I've never seen you wear those at school. Are they part of your work uniform or something?"

Here's something I can answer. I hold them up and explain. "Not exactly, well, sort of," I answer.

"Well that clears that right up," Jen laughs.

"Ok, here's left," I say holding up my green wrist band, "And here's right," I hold up my right arm. When ships have lights they put the green light on the left and the red light on the right. Two ships approaching each other at night are supposed to pass green to green," I say. It feels good to know what to say for a change.

"Oh. Are you a ship person or something?" Jen asks.

"No, not really. It's just that the ship system helps me with my dyslexia. I have trouble telling left from right. And they come in handy when I'm delivering pizzas 'cuz I skate all over going to lots of houses, sometimes right, obviously, sometimes left."

"Oh, I get it. Pretty smart," Jen says, smiling. We stand there looking at each other for what seems like forever until Jen asks "So? Are you done working? Can we go?"

"Oh, uh, yeah, I think so, but let me ask," I tell her. "Can you wait a second while I ask Joe?"

"Sure," Jen says. "I'll pack up my stuff."

I head to the back. I usually would just yell something to Joe, but I need a minute, so I walk into the back. Joe and Jorge are both back there, standing completely still, doing nothing, super quiet, which they never are, and they both smile huge when I come in.

"What's her name, Man?" Jorge asks. "She seems real nice."

"Yeah, Bro, what's her name? You meet her at school?" Joe asks.

I try not to smile, but that's hopeless. "Her name's Jen," I tell them, "and yes, she is nice. Can I go now, Joe?"

"Who am I to stand in the way of love?" Joe says waving a spatula like he's conducting an orchestra. "Of course you can go, Romeo. Would I stop you?"

Give me a break!" I tell him and then, "Thanks. See you tomorrow."

"15 minutes early," says Joe. "You promised."

"I won't forget. Thanks!"

"Take care, Chris," Jorge says.

"Thanks, Joe. See you Jorge."

Jen and I skateboard along the streets and sidewalks, trading the lead. Sometimes we talk and laugh loud, other times neither of us says anything. It's weird. I've skated with plenty of friends, and kids I didn't even know at a skate park or wherever. I never noticed before now how close I can come to someone without knocking them over, or how fun it is to weave in and out of someone else's path. It used to be that when I skated with someone it was more of a competition thing. Like I can do this, can you, or have you tried this yet? Jen and I weave and talk, talk and weave. I'm not really doing any tricks, and she's not asking me to show her any tricks. We're just hanging out, on skateboards.

And then suddenly Jen says, "Come on! This way. I want to show you something." She veers off down a street, so I follow. I immediately recognize where she's going. Sure enough. We're at the new skate park.

"See? It just opened," Jen says as she steps off her board in front of the skate park.

"Yeah, I know," I tell her. "I saw it the other day. It looks pretty amazing. Have you been inside?"

"Oh," she says. She sounds sort of disappointed that I already knew about it, which made my face get hot again. "You've already been here?"

"Well, sort of. Just once though."

"Well, I haven't, so no, I haven't been in. Wanna go in and check it out?"

"Sure," I say and head on in.

The first thing I notice is the sound of skateboards landing, guys shouting at each other, and then, suddenly, loud music. Then I notice a huge poster in the lobby. "Midwest Invitational! Featuring Dakota Servold, Ryan Sheckler, and Mike Mo and Westside's Own Frank 'Wheeler' Parks!" it says. On the left side of the poster there are photos of all four in the middle of "Amazing tricks!'" Jen notices the poster right away, and as she stares at it, Shido eyes her.

"Look!" she says to me, pointing at the poster. I can't tell whether she's impressed or surprised.

"If he's so good, why is he such a jerk?" I mutter.

"Trust me. He didn't used to be that way," she says, seemingly more to herself than to me. She turns to look at me, not the poster. Then she turns to Shido and asks, "Mind if we look around?"

"Sure," Shido says, "Five minutes. No skating for him though. Unless he wants to pay. You, little lady, you can skate as long as you like."

Oh, that's okay. We won't skate, I just want to look around for a minute."

Shido gives her a creepy smile which we both laugh at as soon as we move away from the lobby and head through the doors into the park.

Like the last time I was here, there are a lot of people here. It's hard to recognize anyone with everyone wearing a helmet and tearing around. Two in particular seem to be trying to outdo one another. Jen notices at the same time.

I'm just thinking how sweet this park is and how much time at Joe's translates into how much skating time here, when I hear, "Well look who's here," and Vert and Grinder glide past and then speed up, heading toward the half pipe. I look at Jen and she looks pissed. I'm pretty sure she's not real thrilled to see Vert and Grinder. We both know Wheeler's got to be here too.

"Come on," I say to Jen.

"No, I'm fine. They're just idiots," she says. And then we both watch them for a while. "But I really gotta say, I didn't know these guys were that good," Jen adds after a couple of minutes.

I'm impressed too. In fact, I'm so impressed I forget to be pissed at Vert and Grinder for being such jerks. "Wheeler's even better," I say as I suddenly notice that it's Wheeler who is one of the few kids who's successfully landing the half pipe. We both watched an amazingly fast flip Wheeler just barely pulls off.

"Yeah. I know," Jen says real quiet.

Finally I come out of my trance. "Come on, let's go," I tell her and look toward the doors.

"Going someplace?" Wheeler says and steps off his board real close to Jen.

"Just leaving, actually," I say.

"Hi Frank," Jen says. This is the friendliest I've seen her with Wheeler since I met her.

"Jennifer," Wheeler says grinning.

I'd really like to not be here, but my shoes seem stuck.

"Been skating together?" Wheeler says, staring straight at me.

"Yeah. You never took me skating," Jen says to Wheeler.

Wheeler finds this funny somehow. "We did other things," he says like a complete idiot.

Jen is not laughing now and she seems to come out of a trance. "You're right, Chris. It's time to go." She starts to stomp past Wheeler, but he grabs her arm.

"You don't miss me?" Wheeler says, pulling her closer to him.

"I miss the old you, Frank. The one from fifth grade. Remember him? He was a nice. Not rude or mean. Not like you. Let go, Frank," Jen says, trying to yank her arm away.

"Let her go, Wheeler," I say. I seriously don't want to get in a fight with this dude, but I will if I have to.

"Oh ho! Retard speaks! How 'bout some poetry, Professor?" Wheeler says real loud so a couple of kids nearby turn toward us.

I am so sick of this jerk. I drop my board and put my full

weight behind a shove. Wheeler lets go of Jen, stumbles backwards, regains his ground and then comes back at me. I ready myself to slug Wheeler across the jaw. Wheeler comes at me, pissed, and then Jen somehow gets tangled up in the shoving, and then I'm on the ground and Wheeler's on the ground and then I hear Jen scream. I look toward her and see that she's fallen against the doors and she's holding the side of her head.

"Look what you've done, you retard!" Wheeler yells and jumps up and stumbles to Jen. She's bleeding and the blood runs through her fingers. Wheeler is looking around desperate for something to put on Jen's head, can't see anything, takes off his shirt and wraps Jen's head carefully. A crowd has slowly started to gather around the two of them and I am completely paralyzed. I don't get up, I don't go to help Jen. I don't defend myself and scream that if it weren't for Wheeler, none of this would have happened. I just sit there like the moron Wheeler says I am and watch.

I watch Wheeler help Jen and I hear him whispering "Don't worry, Jen. You're going to fine." And then Wheeler yells "Quick you idiots! Get some help!"

Shido comes running, sees the blood and runs back to the lobby. Someone hands Jen a towel which Wheeler wraps over his shirt.

I am still completely helpless. I'm starting to get really mad, but then I'm really worried for Jen, but she doesn't need my help. I'd just look like an idiot again trying to help.

"I'm ok! I'm ok. I think," Jen says quietly.

"That's a lot of blood. She needs to go to the hospital," some kids in the crowd say.

Shido returns with ice and a paper towel roll which he points at me, "You! Out!" he yells.

"But, I wasn't, it wasn't me," I say, and all the people in the crowd ignore me.

"I don't care what you did or didn't do. I told you to get out. Now, kid," Shido says. He's getting mad. Probably because his brand new skate park now has blood on it.

I get up, grab my board and try once before I leave. "Jen, I didn't mean…?"

"We'll look after her, Shido. We'll make sure she gets home," Wheeler interrupts me. He's ignoring me and looking at Shido while he helps Jen get up. "My brother can get us to the hospital, no problem. And sorry about the mess. It's a shame your new skate park had to get messed up because some idiot wanted to fight," Wheeler says this and nods his head my way.

Shido nods to Wheeler and tells him, "No problem. I'll take care of this. You just get her to the hospital." Shido then turns to me, looking like he's ready to push me out the door. I go before I can make an even bigger fool of myself. I skate around the corner of the building and watch Wheeler, Vert, and Grinder walk with Jen who is still holding the towel to her head. I really hate those guys. I wish I could just beat the crap out of them in front of everyone at school. I wish I could just show everyone what jerks they are. But I know I won't do any of that. I watch Wheeler's brother pull up, watch the rest of them help Jen into the backseat, and then I watch them pull away.

CHAPTER TEN

I take the super long way home thinking about Jen, and Wheeler and the skate park and Joe. So many different things are swirling around in my head I almost miss my street. When I finally roll down my street I have to stop short so I don't roll past my house. I kick up my board and walk up the front walk and up the four steps into the house.

Just before I open the door I see my mom reading in the living room. I am in no mood for her 20 questions, so I make a run for the stairs and my room.

"Chris?" she calls. I know I can't outrun her, but I'm hoping she's not in one of her moods where she doesn't give up until I tell her every detail of my day. I shut the door to my room, but not real loud, otherwise I know she'll be up here in a second

It's no good. I hear her coming up the stairs about ten seconds after I shut the door. "Chris? You know I want you to at least say hello when you come home. What's going on? Has something happened?" my mom asks. She's at my door, sounding like she's ready to stay there until she gets some answers.

"I want to go back to Kennedy," I tell her.

"Oh, Chris," she says and takes a big, long sigh. "Look. It's Friday. We have the weekend - two days to think about it. If you still feel the same way on Sunday night, well, then, we can talk about it. But, Honey, school was hours ago. You've been at work. Did something happen at work?" She sounds suspicious, like she knows there's a story that I'm not telling.

"No, no. Nothing happened at work. I'm ok, Mom. I'm just tired. Ok?" I am suddenly really tired, like fall on the bed and pass out for three days tired. The last thing I want right now is a long heart to heart. "Can we talk in the morning?"

She waits a while before she answers, "Ok, Honey. Do you have homework?"

"A little, but I have the whole weekend to do it and I'll do it, I promise."

"Ok then. Are you working tomorrow?"

"Yeah, at 11. 11-4."

"Ok. Well, you better get to bed and get your rest then. Good night."

"Good night, Mom," I say. I'm relieved she let me off the hook, at least until morning. I have a lot I got to figure out. I fall onto my bed without even taking off my shoes and sleep.

———

The next day, Saturday, I wake up feeling fine until I remember what happened at the skate park. As I'm getting dressed I go through all the details again, how Wheeler shoved me then I shoved him. I can't remember exactly how Jen got in the middle of it and how she got so badly hurt. I mostly remember feeling stupid and how Wheeler made me feel like the whole thing was my fault. I want more than anything to stop thinking about it. I'm glad I have to work today. Maybe that will get my mind off it. I grab a super quick breakfast and toss my board down the steps.

"Don't want to be late for work! See you later, Mom!" I yell as I see my mom walking into the kitchen with a cup of coffee.

"Well, ok. Have a good day!" she yells back and waves from the door.

I smile to show her I'm fine. "See you!"

"Bye," she says, but she looks suspicious, like she knows I'm hurrying just to get out of talking to her. "See you when you get home!" she adds, making sure I know that we will talk, eventually.

I get to Joe's, and just like I was hoping, today is going to be a busy one. There's a big football game on TV and that means lots of pizza. When I'm not delivering pizzas, I'm cleaning up the dining room. Just as I am sweeping up after the lunch rush, in walks Wheeler, Vert, and Grinder. What started out as a good day suddenly has gone really, really bad.

"This is where you work, huh?" Wheeler says, looking around.

I think to myself, now who's the idiot? Do you think I sweep this place because it's fun? But I keep my thoughts to myself.

"Jen called me and told me she's going to be ok by the way. Nothing serious," Wheeler says, still looking around, not looking at me. "No stitches or concussion or anything. Head wounds bleed a lot, but she's fine," Wheeler says, finally looking at me, well, mostly at my apron which now I realize I look like an idiot wearing.

Joe comes out of the kitchen pretending like he's reading a newspaper. He stands in the back of the dining room, leaning against the back counter, like he's not paying attention to us. I can tell he's watching me, though, seeing how I react to what Wheeler's telling me.

"Anyway, she wanted me to let you know so there's no hard feelings. She's says she'll see you in school, but probably not outside of school, if you know what I mean. Pizza here any good?" Wheeler asks.

"It's the best," Joe says, and folds up his newspaper. He doesn't look like he'd like them to stay and eat though.

"Cool. We'll have to come back and get some sometime," Wheeler says. Just before he pushes the door, he turns around, "Don't mess with stuff you don't know about, Reynolds. Just some friendly advice." Wheeler pushes the door and leaves, Vert and Grinder close behind.

"Who the hell was that?" Joe asks nodding toward the door.

"Just some kids from school," I say and pick up my broom.

Joe shrugs and goes back to his paper. "He seems like a real jerk to me," he says and then looks back at the paper and says, "Hey, wait a minute."

"Wait for what?" I say.

"I was gonna show you this." He hands me the folded paper and points to an ad. "Is that him? Is that that kid who was just in here?"

"Yeah, I know all about the competition."

"Well, are you gonna do it?" he asks looking at me.

"What?" Joe has some crazy ideas for sure, but this one is off the charts.

"This! The Westside Invitational!" He's jabbing the paper with his finger. "Jeez. For a bright kid, you sometimes take a minute to catch on," Joe says shaking his head at me.

"Give me a break, Joe. I'm not that good. I can't compete in that," I tell him.

"The hell you aren't! I've seen you. And if there's one thing I know, it's skateboarding, and well, pizza, and you're that good," Joe says, practically yelling.

"Come on, Joe. Besides. I couldn't do it even if I wanted to. It says 'Invitational'. Do you see my invitation anywhere?" I start looking around the dining room.

Joe throws his arms up, "Suit yourself, Kid. You don't have to do it. You don't have to show other people how good you are. You don't have to show that jerk who's obviously giving you a hard time and who obviously has a history with that girl who was in here and who obviously needs to be taught a lesson about being a complete jerk." Joe is now definitely yelling. Good thing there aren't any customers around.

"No offense, Joe, but it's none of your business," I say. I really don't want to tell Joe the whole story. I don't even want to think about it.

"Fine. But if it were me, and I knew I could beat him, I'd be out there every day practicing, getting my tricks down just right so I could ram my board down his throat. Especially if it had something to do with a woman," Joe says, smiling a little and bouncing his eyebrows.

"I think you need anger management classes, Joe." He's cracking me up now. "You don't even know what you're talking about."

"Oh I don't, don't I? What I know is that there was a pretty girl in here who waited a half hour for you to finish work so that she could skate home with you. And I know that some lughead kid came in here talking about some girl that you need to stay away from. Do I have it right so far?" Joe asks.

"No, I mean yes, I mean, sort of, but you don't know the whole story – Joe! I can't skate in the Invitational. There's no way!" Now I'm yelling.

"Even if it meant you'd have the chance to ram your board down that kid's throat?" Joe asks.

"It doesn't matter if I want to or not, Joe, I can't skate in it. Besides, you didn't always skate when you had the chance. You stopped," I'm getting mad and I want Joe to leave me alone with all his stupid crap about me skating in the Invitational.

"I guess you're right. I did stop. Maybe I missed my opportunity. But you – you have amazing skills. If I had a son I'd like him to be just like you, only I'd want him to be more of a fighter, someone who wouldn't back down, especially if he had an opportunity to do the world some good by putting a jerk in his place," Joe said and slammed the paper down on a table and stomped back to the kitchen.

CHAPTER ELEVEN

The next Monday I walk into Ms. James' office, and plop down in the chair and drop my backpack. She's on the phone, but gives me a shocked look, partly surprised and partly irritated.

"Let me call you back," she says to whoever's on the phone. "You're interrupting me," she says to me looking kind of pissed.

"I have to write a frigging report for Health."

"So? Is that a reason to be rude?" she asks me.

"So I hate Health and I hate reports and I have to write a Health Report," I say back.

"Well, I hate reports too. I hate rudeness even more," she says and then waits for me.

I take a deep breath. "Sorry. You're right. I was rude, but I still hate Health and writing reports," I say. I like Ms. James. I really don't want her mad at me.

She looks me over to see if I mean my apology, and then finally she smiles a little and asks "What did you do at Kennedy when you had to write reports?"

"We didn't have to," I tell her.

"I see. Tough school," she nods.

"I can't read and I can't write. Now what do I do?" I say. She's like the only person in this school who I would say anything like that to.

"First of all, neither of those things are true. Maybe Ms. Ellis will let you give your report orally."

"In front of class? No thanks. Did that already. Not fun. Actually not fun for me. Everyone else seemed to think it was very fun, or funny anyway," I say, remembering that very long and embarrassing day in English.

"Maybe that's the point," she says, sort of to herself. She

stops for a moment, thinking.

"What? What's the point of what?" I ask, completely lost.

"Humor is a great way to communicate. People remember, that's for sure. And humor keeps everyone loose, including the speaker. As long as you're not being laughed at, that is. If you are in charge of the humor, it can be very effective," she says smiling like she's discovered something.

"Uh, I think I get it, but I don't see what this has to do with a Health Report."

"Well, keep your mind open to new and unusual ideas for your report, I will too. Between the two of us, we ought to come up with something that will be not just possible, but maybe even fun for you," she says.

"Ok..." I say, feeling very doubtful.

We get to work on reading exercises and go over last week's stuff. She leaves me to fill out some worksheets while she takes a couple of calls. After about a half hour she tells me "Ok, now I'd like you to recite these words in their exact order for me," and she hands me a sheet of paper.

I look at them for a second before I start. "Wait. These words? This is Kindergarten stuff," I say and try to hand the sheet back to her.

"Humor me," she says, tapping the paper with her pencil.

"Fine. I...a...winner...am."

"Good. Now unscramble them and put them into a sentence."

"I...am...a...winner. So? Big deal," I say.

"Stick with me now," she says. "Write the sentence in the air with your finger."

"You serious?" I ask. This sounds very weird and stupid. I do it, but I'm not real happy about it. "There," I say as I put a period at the end of my air sentence.

"Good. Now. Close your eyes. I want you to picture yourself in the sentence."

"What? I don't get it. Picture myself how?" I ask. My eyes are open now.

"No, no. You have to keep your eyes closed. Picture yourself winning something, something really important to you, the best thing you could ever imagine yourself winning." She sounds super excited. It's hard not to crack up. "Got it? What do you see? What are you winning?"

"Uh, I don't know. I can't think of anything I want to win," I say. I really do start trying to think of something, but I'm coming up with nothing.

"Come on! Be creative!" she says.

"Ok, ok…Uh, I see me skateboarding and leaving a trail of the words behind me in cursive. That creative enough?" I say, opening my eyes to see her smiling huge at me.

"That will do," she says. "Now close your eyes again!"

I do, again, and I hear her get up, walk out of the room and then right back in again real quick. She's rolling or pushing something like a cart toward the table.

"Now open 'em," she says.

I open my eyes just in time to see Ms. James pull a plastic cover off of a machine and yell "Voil'a!"

"What's that?" I ask. It's a machine, and it's on a cart, but I have no idea what it is or what it does.

"Chris, meet Mr. Kurzweil," Ms. James says, sweeping her hand like she's introducing two kings to each other.

"Ok…" I say, still not a clue.

"Can I borrow a book?" she asks, nodding toward my backpack.

"Sure," I say and give her the first thing my hand hits: Robert Frost.

"Thank you," she says and then she slides it into the machine. Then, in a computer-voice, the machine says, "The... complete...works...of...Robert...Frost."

"Woah," I say. This is weird. Cool, but weird.

"Pretty neat, huh?" Ms. James says.

"That thing just read the cover of the book? Seriously?" I ask her.

"Yep. It's a machine that reads. Pretty cool. It can help you a great deal," she tells me.

"Yeah, I can see that! How is this even possible?" I ask her, leaning closer to the machine, trying to get a better look at something on it that will tell me how it can read.

"Well, I'm not going to pretend that I understand all the mechanics of it, but what I can tell you is that this machine – I like to call it Mr. Kurzweil – has been an enormous help to a lot of people with dyslexia, and I think it can help you too," Ms. James says, watching me check out the machine. "What do you think? Want to try it out? Want to see if it will help you?"

I shrug and say, "Sure." I'd love to mess around with this machine. I want to figure out how it works. If I just have enough time, I can probably figure it out.

"That's what I was hoping you'd say," Ms. James says, and then she takes my Robert Frost book out of the machine, puts it in back on a stack of books that are sitting behind the machine - or Mr. Kurzweil - on the cart, then pushes the whole thing toward me and tells me "See you next week."

"What? Wait! Next week? What do I do? I don't know how to work this!" I say, but really I'm kind of excited to have a whole week to check this thing out.

"Don't worry. I know you'll figure it out," she says, smiling, and then she leaves, just like that.

CHAPTER TWELVE

It took me only a couple of days to figure out Mr. Kurzweil. It's a sweet machine, amazing really. I go through book after book. At first the computer voice cracked me up because it sounds so weird, but I got used to it. I start to see Ms. James' point about Mr. Kurzweil being able to help me in school. With Mr. Kurzweil, school might just be possible. I even get it to read some of Robert Frost's poems over and over.

About a week after I figured out Mr. Kurzweil, I'm sitting in the back of Hess' class, as far from Wheeler as possible. I also just happen to be three rows directly behind Jen. Hess is droning his usual drone.

"Now, listen to the way Mr. Frost puts the words together: 'Yet knowing how way leads on to way, I doubted if I should ever come back. I shall be telling this with a sigh. Somewhere ages and ages hence: Two roads diverged in a woods, and I - I took the one less traveled by, And that has made all the difference.'"

Hess lets out this big sigh and stares at us, expecting what I don't know. I like the poem, I really like it in fact, but Hess has a way of making me think about hating it. No one is saying anything which clearly makes Hess mad.

"Perhaps poetry is a learned passion. Perhaps middle school students aren't able to understand Frost's challenge to his reader to see life as a series of choices we make and that making the harder, less popular choice can sometimes lead to great things," Hess says. He sounds like he's trying to control his anger, but he can't fool me. It's plain that he wants someone to drop to the floor with the beauty of the poetry or whatever.

"I see that in the poem, Mr. Hess," says Lindsay who is

sitting by the door. "And I agree. Sometimes it's harder in the short run to do what is not popular, but in the long run it's the best choice," Lindsay says smiling.

"That's very astute, Lindsay. Thank you for saying that so eloquently," Hess says, happy at last. And then the bell rings.

I watch Jen walk out of the classroom and I follow. I feel a little creepy following her. We haven't really talked since she fell at the skate park, and, while I know it's not my fault, I still feel like I should apologize or something. Jen heads to the cafeteria and sits with her friends, and I am back to sitting by myself. I watch them for a while, trying to think of what to say, how to begin a conversation with Jen, but before I can even get a decent opening line together, lunch is over and Jen and her friends take off, headed to fourth hour. I toss my lunch bag away and head off to see Ms. James. Seeing her is quickly becoming what I look forward to the most.

———

I go to Joe's right after school. I got the Thursday dinner shift. I drop my backpack, say hello to Jorge and Joe, and am immediately handed the Thompson's usual Thursday pizza to deliver to their house three blocks away.

I say, "Hi, Mr. Thompson, I've got your pizza," to Mr. Thompson like I say every Thursday.

Mr. Thompson says, "Hey there, Chris. Pizza's here, everybody!" like he does every Thursday, and then he gives me my usual $15.00 - $12.99 for the pizza and $2.01 for me.

I tell Mr. Thompson, "Thanks a lot, Mr. Thompson. I appreciate it," like I do every Thursday, and then I head back to Joe's.

I'm skating back kind of slow thinking I could go to the

Thompson's, deliver their pizza, collect the money and make it back to Joe's with my eyes closed. I bet I wouldn't let one pepperoni slice slide. I don't try my usual jump over the trash cans. I'm mostly just bored and still haven't figured out what to say to Jen, how I can make everything go back to how it was before she hurt.

"Hey, what's wrong with you?" Joe says watching me roll into the parking lot super slow as he's taking out a bag of garbage.

"Nothing. Why?" I say, stopping and kicking my board up.

"Oh, there's something wrong, all right. You've been moping ever since your shift started. And you didn't even try your jump," Joe says nodding toward the row of trash cans at the side of the building. "Don't tell me nothing's wrong."

"I don't want to talk about it," I sigh, feeling like my sigh sounds like Mr. Hess'.

"Suit yourself," Joe says shrugging. "Got something for you, though. It's inside," Joe says grinning.

I know that look. He's got something up his sleeve, but I'm really not in the mood. I slowly go inside and look around. Nothing looks different to me. I'm about to say so when Joe comes from behind me and jabs his finger at a newspaper sitting on a table.

"Read it," he says.

"What is it?"

"Just read it," Joe says again, jabbing the paper harder.

It's a copy of the poster for the Invitational I saw at the skate park again, only this has a form on the bottom to fill out for people who want to sign up to skate.

"So?" Joe says, staring at me.

"Joe, we've talked about this already, remember?"

"Well, aren't you gonna fill it out?" Joe asks like he didn't hear what I just said.

"It says right here, Joe: In-vi-ta-tion-al," I say, pointing to the big black letters across the top. "I don't have an invitation to skate in this."

"I got your invitation," Joe says with that grin of his.

"What? How? How do you have an invitation for me?" I say.

"Aw, it's easy. Just talked to 'em," Joe says, shrugging it off.

"Yeah, but I never said I wanted to skate in this," I tell him. "Besides, I can't compete against those guys, Mo, Sheckler, and Servold – those guys are amazing."

"I know you want to skate in this, Chris. And those aren't the guys you have to compete against," Joe says looking suddenly serious.

"What? What are you talking about? You mean there are better guys skating in this? Better than those three?" I say, looking at Joe like he's nuts.

"Parks and -" Joe jabs me in my chest, "you! Those are the two you have to watch out for."

"Now I know you're nuts, Joe. I can't beat Wheeler either. And I have no idea what you mean that I have to beat myself. You sound like you're losing it, Joe," I tell him. "Anyway, the guy that runs the skate park probably wouldn't let me skate there let alone in the Invitational. I had kind of an incident there," I tell Joe who does not look convinced. In fact, he doesn't even look like he's listening.

"Tell me all about it on the way," Joe says and quickly folds up the paper, grabs my arms and steers me toward the back door. "Leave your backpack here. We won't be long. Jorge! Cover for me, will you? Chris and I have an errand to run!" Joe is yelling and pushing.

I hear Jorge call out, "Ok, Boss, see you in a bit," and then before I know it, I'm sitting in Joe's van heading out of the parking lot and down the road.

"I'm starting to get worried about you, Joe," I say, buckling up before we can get pulled over by a cop. "You're acting like a crazy man."

"Call me crazy, just don't call me late for dinner!" Joe practically giggles and turns left onto to street where the skate park is. I can't help it, I laugh. Joe's nuts, for sure, but he's a lot of fun.

"So, I should tell you about what happened at the skate park," I tell Joe while he's fiddling with the radio.

"Not now, my man, this is my song," Joe yells and turns up the radio and starts drumming on the steering wheel. By the time we get to the skate park, the song is over and I've told Joe nothing about what happened.

We pull into the parking lot, and Joe is out of the van and at the door practically before he slams it into park.

"You're gonna kick butt!" he yells over his shoulder just before he pushes the door open. I jog to catch up and hesitate at the doors to the skate park for a second.

"What are you waiting for? An invitation? Ha!" Joe says, holding the door open for me with one hand and pulling my shirtsleeve with the other. "Come here. Check this out."

He lets go of me and we walk over to the trophy case.

"See? Wouldn't you like one of these? I can see the engraving right now: 'Chris Reynolds, 1st Place.'" Joe says, putting his face close to the glass.

"Yeah, right," I say. It's like he totally forgot that I wanted to tell him something. Listen, Joe," I start again, and then Shido appears.

"I thought I told you to get outta here. That also meant don't come back," Shido says staring at me and looking very pissed off.

"Hey! What's going on here?" Joe is suddenly out of his

trance and stepping between Shido and me.

"Come on, Joe. Let's go. I knew this wouldn't work," I say, but Joe's doesn't move. And now Shido looks like he wants to take on Joe too.

"Who are you?" Shido asks Joe. "Do you know this kid? He's banned from my skate park," Shido says. He's not backing down. Shido definitely outweighs Joe, but Joe's pretty wiry. It would be a good fight – a good fight that I really don't want to witness.

"I told you, Joe. Let's just go. Please," I say and now I'm pulling on Joe's shirt.

"Yeah, I know this kid. I'm his sponsor for the Invitational. You the guy I talked to on the phone?" Joe asks, calming down a little.

"I'm Shido. This is my skate park. You're Joe Wheaton? And this is the kid you're sponsoring?" Shido says, deflating a little and looking more closely at Joe. "I remember your Invitationals. I was at a lot of them. You were a sweet skater back in the day," Shido adds. Now he's definitely losing his interest in punching Joe.

"Yeah I'm Joe Wheaton. Glad you remember. Glad anyone remembers, actually. Now I own Joe's Pizza just a mile west of here. Ever been?" Joe says, putting out his hand to shake Shido's.

"Oh, yeah. I know the place. Didn't know you owned it of course. I've ordered pizza from there, never ate in though. Good to meet you, Man," Shido says. Now he's actually smiling – smiling and shaking Joe's hand. I breathe a sigh of relief. Maybe Joe's the ticket in getting Shido to forget about the whole incident.

"This is the kid you're sponsoring?" Shido asks, nodding my way.

"Yep. This is him. He's a good kid. A really good skater, too,"

Joe says, and suddenly I blush.

"You ever competed before?" Shido asks me. It's like he's forgotten about the whole scene from last week.

"Sure! He's from California," Joe says jumping in before I have a chance to say anything. I have no idea where he got this idea, but Joe seems so sure, I half believe I am from California.

"Right, well, it's three events," Shido says, holding up his fingers and listing them. "There's Street, Vert, and Freestyle. You got the form?"

"It's right here," Joe says, happy as can be, and he hands Shido the completed sheet.

While Shido looks it over, I whisper to Joe. "Joe! What are you doing? I'm not from California! What are you telling this guy? You filled out a form before I even agreed to do this? I still haven't agreed! What are you doing? You can't mess with this guy! He'll kick your butt and then he'll kick mine!" I say, getting kind of pissed that Joe just assumed I'd do it.

"Too late, kid," Joe shrugs. "Besides. It's an investment. You're an investment."

"And if I don't do it?" I ask.

"I lose my money," Joe shrugs again. It's killing me that he's so calm while I'm getting more and more panicky.

"This form is not complete," Shido says, pointing to the paper and holding it out to Joe.

"Not complete? What's the problem?" Joe asks.

"Gotta have a parent or guardian sign."

"Well, that's me. I just must have missed that one," Joe says and takes the paper from Shido and then he tells me, "Turn around, kid. I gotta use your back to sign this."

"Huh?" I ask, but before I can say anything else, Joe spins me around and pushes my head forward and there I am, a human desk. "Uh, Joe?" I try again.

"One second, the man says I gotta sign this, so I gotta sign this," Joe says.

"And the kid's gotta sign too," Shido says.

Joe finishes signing, spins me around again and says, "You're turn, Sport," and then he turns around to be the human desk.

This whole thing is happening so fast, I just sign it without thinking.

"And there you are. All signed by all the right people," Joe says smiling as he takes the paper from me and hands it to Shido.

I know Joe's doing this fast on purpose, so it gets done before I change my mind or think to 'fess up.

"Great, see you at the Invitational," Shido says as he walks away looking at the signed paper.

On the way back to Joe's van I'm still trying to absorb what just happened when something else dawns on me: "How much did that cost, Joe?"

"Not much. Hunnert bucks," Joe says shrugging like a hundred bucks is no big deal.

"A hundred dollars?" I yell, stopping dead in my tracks.

"Well, it would've been cheaper if I entered you in beginner or intermediate, but then you never would've faced that Parks kid," Joe says still walking.

"I'm gonna get creamed," I say, mostly to myself. The reality of this whole thing is starting to sink in. I start walking to the van again.

"No, you're not gonna get creamed. Not on my hundred bucks you're not," Joe says and smiles.

You know you can't really sign for me. It's not legal. You aren't my parent or my guardian."

"Details. Tiny details," Joe says, waving his hand like he's shooing away flies. "If I worried about details all the time, I'd never be in business. Besides, you're gonna win. I can feel it in my gut."

"Great. You can feel an Italian sausage sandwich too, and that usually means you're gonna be grumpy for days," I say as I reach for the door of the van.

Joe grins at me, and shakes his head. "Just get in."

CHAPTER THIRTEEN

After taking the long way home after school so I can practice some new moves, I glide up my street and notice a strange car parked in the driveway. I come in through the side door into the kitchen. I want to know who's here before I make a grand entrance. I make sure the door doesn't slam and then I creep toward the living room where I hear two voices talking. I stop moving so I can hear who it is. We usually don't have people over. It's usually just my mom and me so it's strange to hear my mom talking to someone else in the living room. I stand as close as I can to the living room without being seen.

"It's been hard, doubly hard because he's so intelligent. It's amazing the way he's figured out how to cope. But I'm afraid he's going to hit a wall someday and he won't be able to cope. All I hear coming out of his mouth is how much he hates school. 'It's boring. It sucks. I'm stupid.' He didn't want to go back to school this past Monday," I hear my mom say. I have no idea who she would say this stuff to. I feel like I should be mad at her for saying all this, but I wait to hear who she's saying all this to.

"Well, I'm glad he decided to return." It's Ms. James. That is so weird. Why is she in my house? And why is my mom telling her all this stuff? Am I in trouble? I try to remember something I did at school that would cause a teacher to come to my house to talk to my mom, but I can't think of anything outside the usual attitude. Is that why she's here? Am I in trouble because I have a bad attitude? I stop breathing so I can hear every word they're saying.

"You know, Cora, I knew there was something unusual about Chris even when he was little. It was when he turned seven that I knew for sure something was different about him. For his birthday his dad and I got Chris a bike. It wasn't assembled. It came in a box. I had hidden it in the garage, but because he was so curious and always looking for new ways to have fun, he found the box in the garage and so we had to tell him that the bike was for him but that his dad had to assemble it first. He seemed happy about the bike of course, but I could tell that we would have a real struggle getting him to wait for his dad to have time to put the bike together. I knew that Chris wanted to put the bike together himself and that, short of locking either him or the bike up, that was what he was going to do. He didn't want my husband to assemble it. 'Can I do it, Dad?' he asked. My husband smiled, looked at me, and well, we both shrugged and said 'Why not? Go ahead. Give it a try.'

We never thought Chris could really do it. We thought he'd try it for a while, maybe 10 minutes before he'd call one of us out there for help. He never asked for help and he had it assembled in about 45 minutes, and what was really amazing was that he never looked at the directions. He looked at the picture on the box, and the next thing we knew he had put it all together. It was unbelievable. He was seven years old. My husband and I just stared at each other and then at Chris. He couldn't read. He was really struggling in school when it came to reading, but he just put that bike together like it was nothing. That's when we both knew that there was nothing wrong with Chris' brain."

"The dyslexic's brain often sees things in pictures. You know, I use this machine, it's called a Kurzweil. Well, I affectionately call it Mr. Kurzweil. It reads aloud. It's a tool kids with dyslexia often find really helpful. I showed Chris once what it did and then I left him to figure it out. I gave him no suggestions, no hints, I didn't even give him the instructions for the machine, and he had it reading to him within minutes. He still has that, Mrs. Reynolds. And you're right. There is nothing wrong with his brain. He is just wired differently," Ms. James says.

"We'd try reading with him, trying to sound out the words, but it was so hard because we are, or we were both teachers. My husband is, I mean was, an English teacher and a poet." My mom's voice got real quiet.

"Chris told me about his dad. I am very sorry. I am sure that it's still very hard."

I hear my mom sigh. "It's been tough, that's for sure. Some days are better than others. I miss having someone I can talk to Chris about, you know? Girlfriends are fine, but no one other than a child's father really wants to hear incessantly about a child. Having a son like Chris is wonderful in many ways, but it did help to have someone to try to figure things out with, you know?" my mom says. She's sounds like she's smiling some.

"Oh, yes. I do know what you mean. It always helps to feel that you're not alone," Ms. James says. And then there's a long pause. I'm trying not to make any sound. I stopped breathing again so they don't hear me, but if someone doesn't talk soon, I'm going to blow my cover.

Finally Ms. James says, "Well, there is good news. After the tests and evaluation, I am confident that we can help Chris cope with his dyslexia. Maybe that will help him like school better. Mr. Kurzweil is a great help, and I've got some other ideas that I think will work for Chris."

I hear my mom say something else, but I've heard all I need to hear. I start to tiptoe upstairs and hear the tail end of the conversation: "I hope so."

"And perhaps that will help him deal with some of his other

issues," Ms. James says. I hear the rocking chair creak which means she's getting up.

"Yes, that would be wonderful, thank you Ms. James. Thanks so much for coming by. Chris is lucky to have you-we're both lucky," my mom says as they walk to the front door, and as I hit the top of the stairs and quietly shut the door to my room.

That night at dinner, my mom doesn't say anything about Ms. James being over, and I don't say anything to her either. She does seem kind of extra cheerful though, and I figure, well, why not? Ms. James is cool. She kind of cheers me up too.

———

Playgrounds, the old ones set in asphalt instead of woodchips are great places to skate when there are no little kids around I grind down the slide, jump to the teeter totter, skating on it while it spins in the opposite direction, and then jump off toward the monkey bars. I try to grind on the monkey bars, knowing I've probably overstepped. Sure enough, just as I land flat on my back I hear a laugh and, "Aren't you a little old to be playing on the playground? I'm pretty sure there's an age limit and you're over by about 5 years!" It's Jen. I jump up trying my best to hide the fact that I'm pretty sure I may have just broken my back.

"Hey," I say, brushing off my sweatshirt. "I may be too old, but I am very immature for my age," I say, smiling.

"Ha, ha. When you do stuff like that, you really should wear a helmet." To my surprise, she looks kind of serious.

"Well, yeah, I guess. They do in competition, but I usually don't. I don't really even think about it. You don't wear helmets in gymnastics and you guys do some pretty crazy stuff," I tell her.

"We have mats we land on, not asphalt. Besides, we have spotters," Jen says. She smiles and loosens a little. "You know, you almost did a Monkey Flip there."

"I almost did a what?"

"A Monkey Flip. It's a move we do or try to do in gymnastics. It's kind of like – well, it's hard to describe. Wait – I'll show you." Jen runs over to a set of bars and climbs up. "Like this." Before I know it Jen is spins on the bar, gaining momentum. I skate over thinking that this is not a good idea after she just cut her head.

"Jen, are you sure?" I'm too late. At the peak of her swing, she swings her legs up in the air, catches her foot with her hand, and flips off in a wobbly dismount just as I show up to catch her, about two seconds too late.

"Woah!" I say, my heart hammering in my chest, really glad that she's not bleeding again and that I am again the cause of it.

"Whew! I wasn't sure I could do it," Jen's breathing hard and really excited.

"Jeez, Jen! You're the one who should be wearing a helmet. Especially with your – If you weren't sure you could d-d-do it, why di-di-did you try?" I'm stammering again. I don't know which question to ask first. I feel sort of mad that she did it, but I'm also amazed. It really was incredibly cool, this Monkey Flip thing.

"I had you to spot for me," Jen says smiling. "Besides, I've practiced it a thousand times."

Suddenly I realize I've got my arms around her waist, "spotting" her, only she's on the ground, no need to keep spotting. Suddenly I'm incredibly embarrassed. I let go and then I remember: "I'm sorry about your head. I feel like such a jerk. I didn't know you–"

"Don't worry about it," she says and heads to the bars again. "Should I try it again? That landing was a little wobbly."

"No! Please, don't! You just got a really bad cut and I feel like it was my fault. I really don't want you to do it again!" I'm practically begging.

"You know it wasn't your fault," Jen says. I'm relieved that she's stopped heading to the bars like she's going to try the flip again. "That's life. Sometimes you get hurt. Life's like that. Happens in war all the time, my dad says." She pauses, looks at the ground and then asks, "You don't have to work today?"

She's talking so fast, and changing topics so fast, I feel kind of lost and so just answer, "Actually, yeah, I should get going. I'm supposed to be there in 10 minutes."

"I'll walk with you," she says, and she walks away from the monkey bars and I calm down a little.

"So who taught you that Monkey Flip thing?" I ask as we head to Joe's.

"No one, really. There was just a group of us kind of hanging out trying stuff, you know, just sort of bored and we came up with the Monkey Flip. It's pretty cool, huh?"

I smile and tell her, "Definitely cool. And you know, you really should wear a helmet. That trick looks super dangerous."

"We had mats in the gym when we were trying it out. You might have a point at the playground though. Just my luck I would fall and I would slice my head open again," she says smiling.

That's when I knew there were really no hard feelings about her hitting her head. I am hugely relieved and glad she isn't mad at me. I skate slowly and Jen walks. We're quiet for a minute or two when I finally say, "I kinda thought you were avoiding me."

"I was avoiding you. But it was for your own good. I figure I was only causing trouble between you and Wheeler. I didn't want to make it any worse for you. I didn't want someone else getting hurt," Jen says, looking at me.

"Getting hurt? You mean me? Or like you again?"

"Let's not talk about, ok? The whole thing was stupid and Wheeler is still a jerk and I'm fine and I'm not mad. Does that clear everything up?"

"Yup. Crystal clear. I'm ok not talking about it, but can I ask one more question?"

"One more and then no more," Jen says, laughing.

"You used to go out with him, didn't you?" I ask.

"You mean Wheeler? Yep," Jen says sighing.

"Still?"

"Huh? Do you mean do I still go out with him? The answer mostly definitely is no."

"So you're not still going with him?" I ask just to be totally sure.

"Absolutely not," Jen says shaking her head and looking very serious.

"And you knew him in fifth grade, is that right?" I ask. I feel like I'm real close to being annoying, but I've been dying to know, and I figure this is my last chance to find out the whole story.

"Yeah. We were in fifth grade. I was a kid. It was stupid kid stuff. What's your point?"

"Well, I'm confused. You told me that you had just moved here last year. If you knew him in fifth grade, did he live somewhere else near where you used to live and then both of you moved here?"

"Oh, I see why that's confusing. I moved back here last year.

We moved away and then we came back. Wheeler never moved away. I did. And that was way more than one question," Jen says smiling.

I smile back, glad that she explained it. We're in front of Joe's, and she says, "Have fun at work. I'll see you tomorrow in school, ok? And hey – careful of flying pizza dough. You might need a helmet," and she giggles, waves and heads home.

"Right! You can never be too careful! See you tomorrow," I say back, watching her cross the street.

"Oh! Chris! Wait! Now I have to ask you a question." Now she's yelling from across the street.

"Yeah?"

"What are you doing on your class project for Health?"

"Haven't thought of anything yet. Should I be worried? Have you started?"

"Ms. Ellis barks, but she doesn't bite. If it's good, she'll give you an 'A'. If it's not, she'll give you a 'C', but she usually doesn't outright fail anybody. I'm going to start mine when I get home. See you!"

"Thanks for the heads up. I'll try to think of something good. Thanks!" I say and wave.

"See you!" Jen waves back and starts to jog home.

───────────────

I had actually totally forgotten about the Health Report. I still wasn't looking forward to it. Whatever Ms. James said about humor sounded good when she said it, but I couldn't yet see how I could use it for the Health Report. I start to slowly skate to the back of Joe's when I look up and notice a guy pasting up a billboard in back of a store two doors down. I stand a minute to watch him on the catwalk with his long handled brush and bucket. I always thought that being a billboard hanger would be a cool job to have. Half the billboard is up. "Public Service Announcement" it says in smaller black letters in the lower left hand corner. The guy is rolling up one half of a guy's face. Above the guy's head are the words "Safe Sex Means Wearing-" I stand there watching and waiting to see exactly how he's going to finish that sentence. I just start to get an idea for a Health Report when I hear "Chris! What are you doing? You're on the clock and I'm not paying you to stare at the sky like you're looking for rain! Get in here! You've got orders to deliver!"

"Oh! Hey, sorry, Joe. I'm coming," I tell Joe.

I go inside and then forget to check on the billboard guy when I start my deliveries. I'm too busy thinking about my idea for a Health Report. I think it's kind of risky, but it definitely is about health. If I think it through, it just might be the best, most memorable Health Report Ms. Ellis has ever seen.

CHAPTER FOURTEEN

The whole time I deliver pizzas that night I'm thinking about my Health Report – what supplies I'll need, how I'll explain it to the class, what props I'll need, when I'll start all the different parts. I try not to think too much about Ms. Ellis' reaction or even if the kids will get what I'm explaining. I'm so caught up in figuring it out that when I finally roll back into the parking lot after delivering my last pizza, I nearly run into Joe before I see him hammering away at what looks like a frame for something really big.

"What the?" I say as Joe looks up, who's unsurprised by me almost running into him.

"You took your sweet time getting back, I see," Joe says. I look around and see that instead of the usual rows of trash cans along the back wall, there's a stack of plywood, two-by-fours, a bunch of tools, and other building materials like nails, screws, and rolls of tape. Joe's on his knees pounding nails. Three sides of the frame look done. I roll to a stop and watch Joe.

"What are you building?" I finally ask him.

"I hope you know how to use a hammer, 'cuz that's what you're going to be doing tonight."

"I just got done with my last delivery. I'm off," I tell Joe.

"Oh no you're not. You're just starting. I need you for another couple hours. But you're not delivering pizzas. I've got Rob coming in to do that. Anyway, he's got a car. Naw, you're gonna be right here, helping me."

"What are we doing?" I ask, kicking up my board and lean it against the wall.

"Ain't it obvious? We're building our own skate park, of course. My investment's gotta practice," Joe says and then stands the finished frame up against the wall next to my board.

"Seriously? Our own skate park? How? What?" I'm trying to put all this together in my head, and then I just give up. "Sometimes I think you're really losing it, Joe, you really are," I say and then I pick up a hammer. I've known Joe long enough to know that when Joe gets something in his head, there's no use trying to talk him out of it. I start asking him questions like, "What's this thing? Some sort of frame?" and "Why all the plywood?" and it's clear he's got the whole thing planned out: jumps, ramps, rails, platforms. I do my best to follow his instructions, yanking my headphones off of my ears when I see his face getting beet red from trying to yell directions to me. We work until the street lights come on. I call my mom to tell her I'm going to work a couple hours over, she says okay, and a couple of hours later, sure enough we get a lot done. It looks like a skate park, and I'm beat.

"Well, there she is, or almost," says Joe. If I'm tired, he looks wrecked. He's destroyed the knees in his pants, his knuckles are raw from hitting wood while he hammered, and he's sweated his way through his shirt, but he looks happy.

"It's going to be sweet, Joe, it really is," I tell him. "Amazing actually."

"Give me a half hour and then you can try it, Joe says, wringing out his shirt.

I am like the walking dead, but there's no way I'm going home without trying it. "Of course, I'm going to try it," I tell Joe and grab my board and drop it. I mess around just outside the park and then, after Joe give me the go ahead, I take off for the half pipe first. It's as smooth as glass. I don't even have to try to move. It's like the half pipe moves me. I forget how tired I am and see-saw back down, and then up again. "This is

89

awesome!" I yell to Joe who's standing watching me grinning ear to ear.

I hop off the half pipe and check out the grinding gear. From one to another I go and then back, and then when I try the higher grind bar, I finally fall. "It's so sweet!" I yell with my fist in the air. "Dude this is unbelievable!"

Joe comes over to where I'm lying and says "Yeah, I think this will work just fine."

"Fine? Fine? This is incredible, Joe. I think this might be better than Shido's" I raise my hand and Joe grabs it to help me up.

"Not quite, Buddy. Your mom is probably having a cow right about now. You should head home," Joe says.

"Yeah, I should. I called her and told her I was working late, but still. I should go," I say. "This is easily my best day at work ever."

"Now when you come to work, you work in the lot. No more delivering pizzas. I gotta make sure my investment pays off," Joe says. "See you tomorrow, Chris."

"See you, Joe. And thanks," I tell him. Tired as I am, I fly home. I can't remember the last time I was this happy about anything.

———

The next Monday at school I think about the skate park at Joe's all day. I'm thinking up new tricks, stuff I could try, stuff that would be impossible but that I want to try anyway. The only time I stop thinking about skating is when I get to Ms. James' and I sit with the Kurzweil machine, or "Mr. Kurzweil" as Ms. James calls it.

"The light of heaven falls whole and white. And is not shattered into dyes...The light forever is morning light. The hills are verdure pasture-wise. The angel hosts with freshness go...And seek with laughter what to brave. And binding all is the hushed snow…Of the far-distant breaking wave." It's reading "The Trial by Existence," which, now that Kurzweil is reading it instead of me or Wheeler or Mr. Hess, I realize, is a pretty great poem. I sit and listen to the end.

"Looks like you and Mr. Kurzweil are getting along," I hear Ms. James say. I'm a little embarrassed. I'm not sure how long she's has been standing in the doorway.

"Yeah. We're buds. Been discussing the nuances of Mr. Robert Frost," I say.

"That sounds pretty heavy," she says smiling.

"Heavy, yeah," I laugh. Sometimes Ms. James cracks me up. "Hey, I've got a question."

"Shoot," Ms. James says, sitting down at the table with me.

"You always work late?"

"How so?" She looks stumped.

"You were at my house the other night," I tell her. "I heard you talking to my mom in the living room."

"You were there? I wish you had said hello. Your mom said you were at work," she says. She doesn't look embarrassed like she was found out or anything, which makes me a little relieved, although I can't really say exactly why.

"I came in through the side door into the kitchen while you were talking. Do you always do that, come to people's homes, I mean?" I ask her. I don't mean to sound mad or anything, cuz I'm not, but I want to know.

"Well, no, I don't always go to students' homes," she says, looking at me real close, like she's waiting for me to say or ask something else.

"I mean, why take the time? And why me? Why did you come to my house and you don't go other kids' houses? For a second I thought I was in trouble," I tell her.

"I can see it being kind of a panicky thing to see a teacher in your living room," Ms. James says. "But you know I wasn't there because you're in trouble, right?"

"Well, yeah, I figured that out, but what I don't have figured out is why you do it. Why do you care so much? Does it have anything to do with your son?" I didn't know I was going to ask about her son. It just sort of came out.

She takes a minute to answer. She's looking away, thinking, and then finally Ms. James says "It might have something to do with James, now that I think about it. Why does anyone care about anyone though?"

"Beats me," I shrug. Now she's asking me something I'm sure I don't have the answer to.

"I guess I don't see what I do as a job. You know, like 'Ugh. I have a job. I have to go to work now.' I happen to like what I do, and I count myself pretty lucky that I do. It's more than a job, really," she says looking at me real close again.

"I get that, I guess. I mean, I like working for Joe's, I don't mind delivering pizzas, but it's not like I think of it meaning anything more than a part-time job to help my mom out with the bills. It's not like I want to do this for the rest of my life."

"Exactly," Ms. James says. "I've also had those kinds of jobs. I worked as a coat check girl at a restaurant, I worked at a fast food place, in college I worked at a clothing store, but none of those jobs were anything I'd want to do forever. This job I have now though at your school at Warren Middle School, this one's different. I think about it a lot even when I'm not at work. I really enjoy it. I like working with the kids, and I try to think of ways I can help them out all the time. And when I think of something and it works, that's an amazing feeling. It feels like I'm making a real difference in a really important way. You know what I mean?" Ms. James is smiling.

"I definitely don't think about delivering pizzas when I'm not at work. Half the time I'm not thinking about delivering pizzas even when I'm delivering pizzas!" I tell her.

Ms. James laughs and says, "Yeah, I think you get it."

"It sounds weird though. Like I can't imagine caring that much about a job," I say.

"You calling me weird?" Ms. James says, looking at me sideways.

"No, not you. Not really. That's not what I mean. It's just that people have been doing some really nice stuff for me lately, and I really don't understand why. I don't get why you would take the time to come to my house, to talk to my mom when I'm not in trouble or anything, just to find out how to help. It seems weird, no offense or anything," I say, trying not to dig myself in even further.

"Well, you ever think that maybe people are being nice to you because you deserve it? Life has dealt you some pretty tough cards. Maybe it's about time for a good hand. I'm glad I'm not the only one being nice to you, by the way. I'd love to hear who else is stepping up."

"Well, there's Joe, he's my boss. He and I just built a skate park for me – not him – in the parking lot of his restaurant, and Jen, well, I guess she's always been nice. I don't know, it's all kind of a bit much, you know?" I trail off and sit thinking but not saying anything for a while, and then I say "Can I ask you another question?"

"Sure. Ask away," Ms. James says, leaning back in her chair.

"What's your son uh, James, right – what's he doing now?"

"My Jimmy? He's in law school. Top of his class too, I'd like to add," Ms. James has a huge smile on her face.

"Really? Wow. That's cool," I say, trying to hide my smile by turning back to Mr. Kurzweil and turning it back on:

"And from a cliff-top is proclaimed," Mr. Kurzweil says, "The gathering of the souls for birth…The trial by existence named… The obscuration upon earth. And the slant spirits trooping by… In streams and cross-and counter-streams…Can but give ear to that sweet cry…For its suggestion of what dreams!"

Ms. James sits with me through the ending of the poem. When it ends she waits a second and then she says, "You know, my Jimmy struggled not just with dyslexia. He struggled most with a lack of self-confidence. For too long he let other people tell him what he could do and couldn't do. Once he figured out that the only one who really knew how far he could go was himself, well, that was it for him. He wanted, he was determined, to see just how far he could go. He really wanted to know his limits. And you know what?"

"What?" I ask.

"He hasn't found the edge yet." Ms. James got up from the table, pushed her chair in and then said "Have you found yours?"

I had no idea what to say, so I said nothing. I just smiled. After Ms. James left, I sat there for a while. So much had been happening so fast lately it was hard to keep track of it all. I thought about Ms. James and her son, I thought about Joe and the park and what he had to do to build it. I thought about Jen and Wheeler and how their relationship fell apart. I thought about my mom and even about my dad and wondered what that all meant. And I even thought about my Health Report and how my plans for that fit into everything that was happening. There was no way I was going to figure it all out before my next class. The bell rang and rattled me out of my trance. I grabbed my stuff and took off toward Math.

CHAPTER FIFTEEN

The day after my talk with Ms. James about finding my own limits and people being kind and all that, I'm standing at my locker getting my stuff to go home when I'm shoved so hard I have to hang on to the locker door to keep from falling. "What the?" I yell.

"Oh. Sorry." It's Vert. Big surprise. And he's smiling.

"Well, if it isn't the little ballerina on wheels," Wheeler says.

The fact that he's still a jerk suddenly threatens to completely blow my circuits. I struggle to not scream and just ram him into the lockers across the hall. "Don't you guys have something better to do?" I say instead, which even I admit is pretty lame, but I really just want to go home before I lose it.

"Just confirming a rumor I heard that you're gonna be skating at the Westside Invitational," Wheeler says, bringing his face uncomfortably close to mine. His breath stinks.

I want to end this quickly, so I nod. "Yep."

"I don't suppose one of your tricks will be reciting Robert Frost while doing a caballerial 360, will it?" Wheeler sneers.

"Not planning on it," I say stuffing my books into my back pack, "but if you do Shakespeare, I'll consider it." One of the things Ms. James says is to use humor, 'It will disarm them,' she's always saying. At this point, I don't care if it 'disarms' Wheeler or not, I just gotta get outta there, fast.

Wheeler laughs. "Oh, a comedian. Well look, Chuckles, I want you to stay away from Jen, ok? She and I are in a rough spot right now, and I don't want you to complicate things. If she wants to talk to you, just walk the other way. Understand?"

I stop packing my back pack and stare at Wheeler. Now

who's the comedian? Who's he kidding? Even I can see Jen is done with him. "Whatever, Wheeler," I tell him.

Wheeler leans in real close again and says. "Understand, Moron?"

"Yeah, I get it. Does Jen?" For the first time, Wheeler's pet name for me does not make me mad. I still can't get over how blind he is. I really thought he was smarter than this. It's kind of amusing to see Wheeler desperate. I almost feel sorry for him.

"Jen? What's Jen got to do – what're you saying, Moron?" Wheeler looks seriously confused. I don't want him to get too confused though. Animals tend to get mean when they feel cornered.

"Nothin' Wheeler. Never mind. Just trying out a joke. Obviously not funny," I say and start walking away.

"I'm sure you'll understand a lot more if I catch you with her," he says and then he heads down the hallway. His goons Vert and Grinder fall in behind and Vert makes a move toward me like he's going to punch me or something, but he doesn't. Instead he jogs a little to catch up with Wheeler and Grinder.

I stop for a second to watch them walk away. For the first time I see Wheeler, Vert and Grinder in a whole new way. They're really just three middle school kids. They aren't tougher or scarier or obviously any smarter than any of the other kids in this school. They're just jerks - bullies who really and truly have nothing better to do than bother other kids. It's how they get their jollies. And Wheeler is just the head bully. Outside of this school they'd be nobodies. Just another group of dumb kids doing their best to mess with other kids for no other reason than it's something to do. Wow. Before I could start feeling sorry for them, I turn back around and head out, toward home.

I think about Wheeler and his goons all the way to Joe's. I'm not making much progress as to why these guys are the bullies and other kids aren't when suddenly I'm there, walking through the kitchen.

"Get to work, young man! There's no time to lose!" Joe yells at me as soon as I come through the door. And then he shoos me with his hand, "Get back in that lot and make it look good!"

It dawns on me that he's not talking about pizza – he's talking about working in the skate park. "Oh, right," I say and grin. "You don't have to ask me twice." I dump my backpack, reach into a cupboard for the helmet, and pull my board out of the straps and toss it out the door I just came through.

I start first this time grinding on the pipes. After about half an hour I start on the half pipe. For whatever reason, this time I cannot make it to the top of the half pipe even after about 5000 tries. "Crap!" I finally yell, and slam my helmet down, pissed.

"Watch your language in my parking lot, young man!" Joe's been standing at the back door for I don't know how long. Fouled mouthed Joe telling me to watch my language is almost as funny as watching Wheeler go after a girl who is clearly done with him.

"Yeah, right, Mr. Potty Mouth," I say. "I suck though. I totally do not understand how I could do this yesterday and today I can't do it at all. What the hell happened?" I am seriously frustrated.

"You know, the problem is that you need more speed on your take-off," Joe says, coming outside and quieting down. "Try shifting your body weight from your pushing foot to your

97

board." Joe's brought the board that I remember seeing in his apartment. "It'll add more thrust to your motion. Give you a better follow-through," Joe says and then he drops the board and makes a move like he's going to skate. "I think it's time for a real lesson." He's on it, and he's moving. "Pumping on a skateboard is like pumping on a swing. To get the swing higher, you lift your legs as you pass through the bottom arc. The faster you go, the higher you can fly up to and off the half-pipe," by this time Joe is yelling to be heard and flying to gain speed.

I manage only a weak "Bust air," but mostly I'm amazed, watching. Joe smiles and goes for a quick tour around the parking lot and then gains an amazing amount of speed in a short distance, pumping just like he said. He crouches down and makes it up the half pipe to and well past the lip, grabbing his board mid-air, and then back down, all casual, no-big-deal-like, like he does this all day long. I stand there with my mouth hanging open.

"Dude," I say. I have never seen Joe skate. Not once has he tried anything on my board. I have been working here, delivering pizzas on my board, for about nine months, and not once has Joe ever told me that he was a skater or that he was an amazing, award-winning skater. I have no idea what to say. "Not bad for an old guy who got his bell rung one too many times."

Joe grins and says, "Naw, not too bad. Still know a couple things. Now you try again, and remember what I said about speed and momentum – just like you're pumping on a swing."

I want to ask him about a million questions like when did he start, who taught him, how many hours a day he practiced, but I can see he's not in the mood for questions. He's already waving his hand at me like, "Go on, go on," so I go. I keep at it. I take Joe's advice. I pump so hard and swing my leg so high

I feel like an idiot, but it works – it really works. And it works almost every single time. I can't believe it. I'm willing to look like an idiot if it means I can nail the half pipe every time. It's an amazing feeling, hitting it every time and not falling once. I shout "Yeah!" the first couple of times, and Joe yells, "Keep your head in it, Kid!" And then I just skate and skate, feeling like this is the closest I've ever come to flying. I stay out there until the only light left is coming from the parking lot lights.

"You should go, Chris. School tomorrow," Joe says at about 9:00, sticking his head out the door.

"Yeah, I know. One more though, let me do it one more time," I say. My shirt is drenched and my legs feel like they've turned to spaghetti, but I want to go one more time.

"Fine. Then out go the lights," Joe says and sits on a crate to watch.

I pump and fly, grab my board and scream down the half pipe. This is the most fun I have ever had on a board. I could do this forever. "Yes!" I yell, "This is amazing!"

Joe shakes his head and yells "That's enough, Bobble-head. Time to go home. This will be here tomorrow. And the day after that."

"And the day after that! Thanks, Joe. I just can't believe it was such an easy fix."

"It 'ain't easy for everybody, just so you know," Joe says, standing in the door. "Now scram before your mother gets mad at me."

"Ok, see you Joe! Thanks!" I yell and wave. I fly home, already thinking about skating after school tomorrow.

———

When I get home I'm completely beat, but I got homework to do so I get out all the stuff for my Health Report and get to work at the kitchen table.

"Hi, Honey," my mom says as she walks into the kitchen. "How was work?"

"Easily the best day ever," I tell her.

"Wow. Good for you. Hungry, or did you get some pizza?"

"Actually, I am starving. I didn't eat any pizza, for once," I say, and I am seriously starved, like I'm going to start chewing on my own arm starved.

"I made a big bunch of pasta. Interested? There's broccoli too," she says, rooting around in the fridge.

"Pasta and broccoli sounds perfect," I say.

"Well, ok then. Give me a second to heat it up and you can eat to your heart's delight."

"Thanks, Mom. Seriously."

"My pleasure, Sweetie," she says and kisses me on my head. "This'll be ready in a minute."

———

In school a couple of days later I'm excited and nervous about the presentation, but something is still missing. I haven't seen Jen in a couple of days, and I'm starting to get nervous about it. I'm making my way to class, when I see Lindsey up ahead and figure she'll know where Jen is. "Lindsey! Lindsey? Hey, Lindsey!" I finally have to yell, it's not so easy trying to get someone's attention in a very crowded hallway.

"Oh, hey Chris," she slows down some to let me catch up.

"Have you seen Jen? She hasn't been in class the last couple of days. Is she sick?"

"No, not sick exactly. She had a bad fall. In gymnastics, but she'll be ok. Hey, do you have your report for Health ready?" Lindsey asks.

"Yeah, I hope so. Gotta give it today. How bad is she hurt?" I'm trying not to sound too eager or desperate or whatever about finding out about Jen, but just then the bell rings and Lindsey takes off.

"Ok, then, see you, Chris!" Lindsey says and disappears in the crowd.

"Wait!" Too late – she's gone. I've fallen plenty of times skating, but never so bad I had to miss school. It's going to take some serious concentration to get through the day. And I have to give my Health Report. Ugh. It's amazing how fast I can go from super happy to crazy depressed.

I practiced at home, alone in my room, but in front of the class, it's just a wee bit different. I waddle into the room and immediately hear some people gasp and a couple of "What the?" One thing I hadn't counted on was the fact that I can just barely see the chalkboard out of the holes I cut into my costume, but the board is pretty big, so missing it entirely seems impossible. Once there, I write "Mr. Condom" on the board and turn around to see Lindsey smiling and Ms. Ellis frowning. Too late to go back now. I take a deep breath and say "My name is Mr. Condom and I'm here to tell you about safe sex." While Ms. Ellis is not too pleased, I do hear people snickering, which is what I'm after – that whole "Disarm them with humor" thing Ms. James talks about.

"Quiet please, this is a serious matter," I say, doing my best imitation of a mean teacher. My voice seems like it's a little muffled, so I speak louder to make sure everyone can hear me. "In many ways, condoms are like people. They have different names." I set up my power point before class, so all I have to do is waddle over to the lectern and find the clicker. I got a whole bunch of great pictures. It seems strange to admit it, but I had a really good time putting this presentation together.

"Rubbers, raincoats, and sheep skins to name a few," I say clicking through a bunch of photos and drawings I spent a ton of time finding on the internet. "And they come in different colors and sizes too, just like people. There are small, medium, large, and extra- large condoms." The snickering is turning into laughter. "Some even have ribs, like Adam." Here I show this great picture of Adam and Eve in the Garden of Eden by Rubens. "Now, if Adam had used a condom, we might not be here today. But that's another matter. Lights, please." Lindsey flicks off the lights while I turn off the projector lamp, and then, my big moment: "Some even glow," I am – or my costume is – a glow in the dark, neon green replica of a condom.

I gotta admit, I love this part. I even hear Wheeler say, "Whoa, Dude, that's awesome" as I do a little turn around to show off my green glow. But I'm not done.

"Condoms can prevent pregnancy and sexually transmitted diseases, such as herpes, gonorrhea, and AIDS. So, in the future, if you're going to play, play it safe and wear a condom. Lights please," I say and Lindsey is there before I even finish the sentence. And then comes my second favorite part: I reach into a bag, pull out a handful of condoms and toss them to the class. "It might seem uncomfortable or even weird to talk about condoms or to ask for condoms at our local store, but it sure beats getting a venereal disease or unwanted pregnancy!" The kids who aren't scrambling to get a condom are clapping and laughing. Ms. Ellis apparently does not want a condom, and she is not clapping or laughing either. Well, you can't win them all, I figure, but I also figure I'll be hearing about my presentation from Ms. Ellis later – in her office. I bow, sort of, and head back out into the hallway and to the bathroom to change. I can still hear the kids laughing and clapping all the way down the hall. Inside the condom costume, I am smiling ear to ear.

───────

My one adult ally in the school, Ms. James, looks none too happy when I stroll into the Resource Room the next day. I don't think I've ever seen her frown. I don't like it much. "What's wrong?" I ask, not thinking for a second that her face has anything to do with my Health Report.

"I heard about your little escapade in Health class. Now you've got Ms. Ellis mad at me because I was the one who suggested you do an oral report." Ms. James tries to sound genuinely pissed off, but she can only pretend for about 20 seconds. "But she'll cool off. Wish I could've been there," she says and then tries to hide her smile.

I'm hugely relieved. I really don't want Ms. James mad at me. "Yeah, it was pretty good if I do say so myself. You know, I kept thinking about your whole 'Disarm them with humor' thing, and I think you're right. It works," I tell her.

"Yes, indeed. It's like people don't expect you to be funny, so they don't know what to do when you are except laugh. It really does soften people, doesn't it?" Ms. James says, smiling for real now.

"Yeah, thanks."

"Not a problem. I did get Ms. Ellis to soften some, not so much with humor as with reason," Ms. James says.

"Reason? So I didn't fail?"

"Not at all. We talked and we decided that while your presentation might ruffle feathers as this is a middle and not a high school, there's probably no better time to talk about the real stuff of sex education than hopefully before kids are engaged in it. It did take some talking, but I do believe you will receive a very good grade on your presentation," Ms. James says.

"Wow. Thanks for that," I tell her.

"There's nothing really to thank me for. The presentation was your idea, your work, your work entirely. I'm really very proud of you. You took a risk in a number of ways, and it worked out. It might not always, but this time it did. You should be proud of that. I know I am," Ms. James says.

"Thanks, I mean, I guess I didn't think of that way. I am glad it's over, I will say that," I say.

"Now there's something more serious going on," Ms. James says, catching me off guard. "Come with me," And just like that, she's at the door. "Let's go, we have to hurry."

"Hurry? To where? Why? Where are we going?" I follow even though I have no idea what's going on.

"To the hospital," she says, hurrying me out the door and down the hall. I have to trot to keep up.

"Hospital? Why? Who's there?"

"Just come on, I'll explain on the way," and with that, we're out the door headed toward her car.

CHAPTER SIXTEEN

"You're the only friend she wanted to see," Ms. James says to me as we head to the hospital. In the car on the way Ms. James tells me about Jen's fall in gymnastics and that she had a concussion and maybe a broken arm. I'm mostly quiet on the way, taking time to understand everything.

We walk into a room with two beds. The first bed is empty, but as I slowly walk in I see feet under the covers of the second bed. It's Jen. I smile weakly and try to hide my shock at seeing her face. She is puffy and red, possibly from crying. Her arm is in a sling outside the covers. She looks small and scared.

"Hey, Jen," I whisper. Ms. James has let me walk in first.

Jen looks at me. She looks so sad I feel I should do something, but I have no idea what. "What happened? How did this happen? Did something happen to make you fall?" I ask all these questions quickly. I'm trying to find the right thing to say, to ask.

Jen shakes her head and squeaks out, "My own dumb fault."

I know it's stupid, but it's like if I could get mad at someone for doing this to Jen, it would be productive, like I could do something about it. And then Jen interrupts my thinking by saying something that completely takes me by surprise.

"I lied to you." She's looking right at me, like she might start crying again.

"What? You lied? About what?"

"Well. I didn't lie, exactly. It's just that that Monkey Flip I did? That was really only the second time I did it. I've been trying for months, and I keep messing it up. I wanted you to think I could do it easily, like it was no big deal. But when I tried again at practice, I fell – really badly."

"I don't get it. Why would you want me to think it was easy?" I am lost.

"I just wanted to be as good at gymnastics as you are at skateboarding, and I tried something I shouldn't have. I just got lucky that the second time I got it right was in front of you," Jen says. She looks so sad. I'm feeling more and more frustrated that I can't think of something to say that will make her smile again. So I just stare at her trying to understand what she's saying.

"Geez, Jen, you don't have to try to impress me…" What she said is finally sinking in.

"I know, I know you don't care about stuff like that, but I wanted you to like me, and I thought you'd be impressed." Jen is starting to sniffle again and I just have to stop her from crying - I have to.

"But I am impressed, or I was already impressed. It has nothing to do with gymnastics."

"Everyone has the right to do stupid things, I just wish they weren't also dangerous," Ms. James says, leaning in toward Jen. I'd forgotten Ms. James was there.

"Yeah, wow, Jen. I'm so sorry you got hurt." I feel so lame, that I don't have any magic words, or I can't make her better or even stop being so sad.

"It's definitely not your fault," Jen says. "It's definitely my fault. I'm so glad you came," and then she smiles. It was a weak, weirdly sad smile, but it's a smile.

"I'm glad I came too," I told her. "Ms. James brought me," I tell her turning to include Ms. James who smiles back at me.

"If you could wrap it up, I would appreciate it," a nurse or someone comes in the room looking like she's very used to kicking people out of rooms, like she's really good at it.

"Oh, ok," I stammer.

"We were just leaving. Thank you," Ms. James says. "It's good to see you Jen. I'm sure you'll be back on your feet and back in school in no time," Ms. James adds and holds Jen's hand for a second.

"Yeah, me too. I mean. I'm sure you'll be fine, right? Back in school. Back doing gymnastics and all that?" I make a half move to hold her hand and then feel weird with Ms. James and the nurse there, so I just sort of pat her hand like some lame grandma and followed Ms. James out. "Bye Jen! See you soon," I say over my shoulder.

"Bye, Chris. Thanks for coming! You too, Ms. James!" Jen says. And then Ms. James and I are walking down the hall. Ms. James pats my shoulder and says "Jen'll be fine. You'll see," right before we walk into the revolving doors to the parking lot.

It feels sort of wrong, but on the way home, my worry about Jen turns into a kind of happiness. Jen was trying to impress me? And then I feel really crappy for being happy. I feel like a jerk, like I'm no better than Wheeler, worse even. At least he was pissed that Jen got hurt. It's all too much to figure out. By the time I get home the "I'm such a jerk" feeling wins out, big time.

———

I really don't want to try to explain it to my mom so I run up the stairs as fast as I can hoping she'll just leave me alone. Wrong again.

"Chris? Is that you? Chris? Joe's trying to get a hold of you, Chris," and just like I knew she would, she heads up the stairs. I close my door and flop face first onto my bed. Closed doors mean nothing to her. "Chris," she's quieter now. I'm in my room, picturing her head leaning in toward the door and her hand on the knob. I feel like a little kid. Maybe if I don't say anything she'll think I'm sleeping and she'll leave me alone. "Chris, are you ok? What's wrong? Did something happen?" When I feel her sit on the bed and her hand on my back, then I really do become a little kid. I start crying. No stopping it. "Oh, Honey, please, talk to me."

"I feel like it's my fault, but I'm not sure how. It's so confusing. Why am I always so confused?" I grab the picture of my dad, look at for a second and then put it face down on the table.

"Oh, Chris" she says, and then she starts to cry too. Great. Now I've hurt two people.

"Can you leave me alone? Please Mom? I just really want to be alone," I say, begging.

"Only if you promise to talk to me later about this, ok?" she asks, sounding desperate.

"Ok. I promise. Just not right now. Not tonight. Please."

"Ok, Honey. We'll talk tomorrow. Good night." My mom leaves, closing the door.

———

The next morning I head to the playground where Jen did the Monkey Flip. I'm really not there to even skate – at least not at first. I guess I'm just sort of drawn there. The more I circle around slowly, though, the more I feel like skating for real. I feel like trying something new, something really hard and dangerous. There's one car in the lot next to the playground and I get an idea. I kick up some serious speed, pumping like Joe does. It feels like my leg might just fly off, but I keep going. I need even more speed than when I'm on the half-pipe. I'm practically flying, crouching, and then I jump. For a split second it really does feel like I'm flying. Then a split second later I'm back on my board with a hard thump. Unbelievably I've cleared the car. It's weirdly silent. No one is there. No one is cheering or saying "Dude! That was incredible!" It's just me, my breath and my board. I slow down and turn back to look at the car. And then I stop and I smile.

That night, after skating most of the day at Joe's parking lot skate park with short breaks to eat and use the bathroom, I roll up to the bona fide skate park and I tell Shido, "I want to skate." Joe follows me to Shido's in his truck and is standing behind me grinning at Shido.

"Go to it, Buddy. You don't need his permission," is all Joe says, and I go into the park. I circle around gaining speed. The other skaters look a little pissed off at me because I'm not taking turns. I'm just doing my own thing, kicking it up. They move off and I launch up the half-pipe perfectly and come screaming back down like it's nothing – like I've done it forever. I come around to do it again, and just as I reach the top I spot Wheeler and lose my concentration for half a second. I wipe out spectacularly, with a loud thud, sliding down on my back all the way to the bottom, my board sliding right into Wheeler's foot. Wheeler laughs and toes it back to me and says, "Figures. Moron." Vert and Grinder are there too, of course, laughing their heads off.

I'm so stunned and pissed at myself I've got no comeback. I just sit there, watching Wheeler and his goons walk away. I sit there feeling and looking like a complete moron.

I take up Joe's offer of a ride back to the restaurant. On the way back both Joe and I are a lot less excited than we were when we were on our way to the park. Just as we're turning the last corner, Joe says, "Well I thought you looked pretty good. Damn good, in fact." He looks at me quickly.

"I suck, Joe," I say real quiet. I can't get Wheeler's stupid grin out of my head.

"No, you don't suck. Straws suck," Joe says, trying lamely to get me to laugh.

"Correction: People suck. Straws are just the instruments through which people suck." I play along as best I can.

"I see. Well, maybe you gotta think of a new trick. Something that hasn't been done before. Something that will really wow 'em," Joe says and pulls into the parking lot, driving past his skate park to the front lot to park his truck.

"I don't think so. I think all the great tricks have already been done," I tell him and get out of the van. I head to the back door to get my ipod and headphones off the kitchen counter. Joe follows me in.

"That all you need?" Joe asks as he watches me wind up my cord.

"Naw, I left my backpack here too. I left it in the back booth. I'll be right back."

"Hurry." Joe fiddles with the bobble-head. "Ready?" he asks when I come back in the kitchen.

"Yeah, no, wait," I say, stopping.

"Huh? What now?"

"Joe, where did you get that?" I ask, nodding to the bobble-head he left bouncing.

"Where'd I get what?"

"That. That bobble-head," I say, pointing at it.

"This? Aw, I was once in this skating tournament in Michigan, competing on a team. I think the name of the team was the Flying Hawks, but we stunk so bad they called us monkeys," Joe says with a grin and gives it another tap to get the head going again. "I keep this monkey bobble-head around to stay humble."

"Give me one more minute," I say and toss my stuff back on the counter and head out the back door. I'm back in again before Joe can catch up.

"Hey, you left your stuff! What are you doing?" Joe says as he and I nearly ram into each other.

"Joe, will you turn on the lot lights?"

"Why? What are you doing?" Joe asks, but he's reaching for the switch.

I head out of the kitchen to one of the back booths and motion Joe to follow. "Come here a second. You're right, Joe. I gotta have a special trick. And I know what it is. Here take this." I hand Joe one cushion and I take another. "It's called a Monkey Flip." I explain with cushions and my hand acting as my board how the Monkey Flip works.

Joe watches, nodding, and asks no questions. I get to the end where I land perfectly of course and Joe says. "Cool. Ready to try it?"

"Let's go," I say, smiling wide. "Mind if we take these outside?" I ask, looking at the cushions.

Joe shrugs and says, "Ok by me, Boss. How many do you need?"

"All we can carry?" I say, looking hopeful.

"Dude, you are half crazy," Joe says laughing, and then, "Here, stack them up in my arms, I'll carry what I can."

We head back outside to the skate park and Joe says, "No, I'm not saying you're not crazy because you might be. In fact, I think you most definitely are, but what the hell." Joe is smiling almost as much as I am.

"I'm going to take that as a compliment. Come over here and spot me, will you?"

"Ok. Now how are you going to start this again?"

"I can't explain it again, I just have to try it. Just make sure I don't break my neck," I say, already circling around to pick up speed.

"Great. I have to prevent a crazy kid from breaking his neck. Right." Joe looks super awkward holding his arms out like he's going to catch me or something. I'd laugh, but I have to concentrate if I have any hope of landing this, so I stuff my laughter down and focus on gaining as much momentum as I can.

I'm heading toward the half-pipe thinking out loud. "I can't remember exactly how she did it, but it was something like this." And I'm off. Before too long, I'm on my butt, half-buried in cushions. "Ow."

"You all right?" I hear Joe ask somewhere above the cushions.

"Yeah, yeah. I'm fine," I answer. "Let's do it again."

"You're the boss," Joe says, grinning.

CHAPTER SEVENTEEN

The next day, Ms. James and I go back to the hospital to visit Jen after school is through. This time I bring some flowers. I'm thinking I might tell her about the skating Invitational if she's feeling better. I'm super excited to tell her, but I don't want to be all excited while she's lying there on her back.

"Why don't you go in first," Ms. James says as we get closer to Jen's room.

I knock softly on Jen's door and then figure I should just probably go in real quiet.

"Who are you?" I say a little loud to some lady who's lying in the bed that Jen was in yesterday.

"Excuse me?" The lady looks a little pissed, and I can't blame her, really.

"Oh, I'm sorry. I didn't mean to be rude. I just came to see…A friend of mine was just here…"

"She left either early this morning or yesterday afternoon. I don't really know. I got here about an hour ago. There was another young man who came by just about 20 minutes ago looking for the same person. The nurse told him he would find her at home."

"Oh, ok, thanks!" I tell the lady and turn around practically knocking over Ms. James. "Did you hear that? Jen's out. That must be because she's doing better! Can we go to her house? The lady just said Jen went home." I don't want to be rude again, but I see no reason to stick around and no reason not to tell Jen about the Invitational.

"Sure, let's go. Thank you for the information," Ms. James adds, waving to the lady in the bed.

"Yeah, thanks, and sorry again for being rude," I add and

then, I pull a daisy out from the flowers and give it to her.

"No problem, young man. Thank you for the flower. That's very sweet of you. Whoever these are for must be quite lucky," the lady says and smiles.

I got no time to lose, so I head out, trying hard not to run.

In the car I'm trying to pay attention to what Ms. James is saying about Jen and how she must be doing better or they wouldn't have sent her home and that sometimes after a bad fall you just need a day or so to regroup or whatever, but I keep thinking about what the lady in the hospital said about some other "young man" coming to see Jen and that this "young man" is probably at Jen's house right now. I know it has to be Wheeler and the more I think about it, the more pissed off I get. Why is it that he had to get there first, that he's going to show at Jen's first making me look like an idiot, like I don't care or forgot about her? I'm getting madder and madder and finally Ms. James says, "We're here, Chris," and she puts the car in park.

I see we're back at school, not at Jen's so it's going to make me even later. But then I think of course we're at school, do I really expect Ms. James to drive me around all day? I feel so mad and confused and ungrateful, the only thing I can get out is, "Oh, yeah, thanks," before I close the car door and head toward, well, I wasn't sure where.

I decide as I glide toward home that the good news I was going to tell Jen is gone, and I toss the flowers and fly to Joe's, not caring who I bump or frighten off the sidewalk. I am so tired of absolutely nothing going my way I could yell until my lungs fried. I screech into Joe's kitchen.

"Joe, I can't do this anymore. I quit," I yell before I even get all the way in the door. I hear nothing. "Hey Joe, do you hear me? I'm done! I quit!" Still nothing. Sighing, I push open the door to the dining room. The lights are all off. Weird. And then suddenly the lights come on and…

"Surprise! Happy Birthday!" Joe, Jorge, Sally, everyone who works at Joe's is there, and so is Ms. James, my mom, and Jen. It takes me what seems like an incredibly long time to figure out what's going on. Slowly I put all the pieces together: There's a banner over a table that says "Happy 15th Birthday!" and there are presents and a big chocolate cake on a couple of tables that have been moved to the center of the dining room "Oh, wow" is all I got to say, and all the anger I felt just a couple of seconds ago just sort of drifts off.

"Happy birthday, Honey!" my Mom says. She's the first one to sort of break the spell. She walks up to me and gives me a big kiss and a slap on the back. "We really got you, didn't we?"

"Oh, yeah. Totally," I say smiling.

"Always thinking about skating, this one is. It's amazing he remembers to eat and bathe!" Joe says and gives me a big hug.

"I thought when I dropped you off at school that I wouldn't be able to get here before you you were going so fast on your skateboard," Ms. James says laughing.

"I think that board is permanently attached to his feet!" Sally says and gives me a hug.

"Seriously!" Jorge adds laughing and shaking my hand.

It's still all sinking in when finally Jen comes up to me and says, "Happy birthday, Chris. I'm really glad I could come," and then she blushes.

"All right, enough of that! Let's everybody eat before the pizza gets cold!" Joe yells and then he and Sally and Jorge start bringing out the pizzas and pitchers of soda. I finally recover some and fully realize what's happening. The pizza is of course my favorite, pepperoni and onion, and there's veggie pizza for my mom. After we all eat Joe imitates my hanging mouth when I first walked in and then my mom announces, "I think it's time for presents! Or should I say 'present'?" and then she brings one present and puts it in front of me on the table. I stare at it thinking the shape looks very familiar.

"Well, are you going to open it or wait for it to hatch?" Ms. James seems as excited as I am about the present.

I start ripping at the paper and, just as I hoped, the Tony Hawk logo appears. "No way! A Tony Hawk! Sweet! This is so awesome! Thanks! Thank you so much!" I look around wondering who I should thank exactly.

"Well, it was sort of a group present," my mom says, looking at everyone.

"Thank you everybody! Seriously. This is the best present ever!" I look at Jen who's smiling from ear to ear.

"You're going to be even better with that," Jen says, and then it's my turn to blush.

"Oh! We almost forgot the cake!" My mom claps her hand over her mouth, but just as she does, Joe comes out from the kitchen singing in his terrible scratchy voice.

"Happy birthday to you!" Everyone joins in and, at the end, Joe sets the cake down in front of me.

"Make a wish!" my mom says.

"Mom, I'm 15, not 5."

"You're never too old for wishes. Now, make a wish, go on!"

I think of the perfect wish, draw a deep breath, and blow. Everyone cheers and I start to cut the cake.

After the cake, singing, and presents, Jen and I manage to find a minute to talk during the party.

"I feel so stupid now. I couldn't believe I did it though! I really did a Monkey Flip! I'm going to do it again, but a lot smarter. My coach said I could tie off so that if I fell, I wouldn't really fall, you know? I guess it seems dumb to be embarrassed just because I tried something hard. Some of the other girls can do it like it's nothing. It comes so easy to them. That can be so frustrating. It's kind of like you and your dyslexia. Now I know what you mean by being so angry when other people can just rattle off words without trying." Jen is talking and eating cake. I polished off my piece about five minutes ago, so I'm just watching and listening, perfectly happy.

I'm sort of stunned by what she's just said, and I don't want the conversation to end. "So, what happens now? When can you start gymnastics again?"

"Well, my doctor said I could start back right away, but I should really take it easy for about six weeks. Just go over basic stuff to get my strength and confidence back."

"I'm really sorry this happened to you. I feel like it's my fault," I tell her.

"Oh, no, it was not your fault, not at all. If I had thought about it, about what kind of a person you are, I would've known that that's not what impresses you. At least I hope that's true…" Jen says looking at me.

"You know that's true. I don't care if you can do gymnastics or not, I mean, it's great that you do gymnastics and I think you're really good, it's just -"

"No, no, I get it," Jen laughs. "Like I think it's great that you skate and you're really good, you really are, but that's not why I like you, I mean," Jen says and I can't hardly believe it. She said she likes me, no doubt about it. Jen officially likes me – me! And then she just about kills me with one of her smiles.

"It really is hard feeling like everyone else is good at something and you're not. I was so angry. I was angry at my mom, at the world, at everything. During the summer when school was out, I used to pretend that I'd never even heard of dyslexia. I was sort of living a lie." Jen reaches over and puts her hand over mine. It's only for a second, but I felt it for hours afterward. Easily my best birthday ever.

———

The week after my birthday I spend mostly collecting bruises. Joe has me at the park every day after school with special permission from my mom to stay after dark. Jen comes by a couple of times to watch and cheer me on. She flinches when I fall and shoots her hands up in the air and yells "Yes!" when I land on my board and not my butt. It was a painful but great week. Joe came out often to watch for a couple of minutes between customers. He even got on his board a couple of times to show me just how to lean or pivot. I really wish I could have seen him when he was competing. The dude must have been awesome.

"How are you liking your new board?" Joe asks when I skate over to him just two days before the Westside International.

"Fine," I say. I'm starting to get nervous the closer the weekend comes, but I don't want Joe to know how nervous I am. I'm trying really hard just to be grateful, to not feel like I want to run out of the park and make up some excuse why I can't compete.

"'Fine'? Your new, sweet, Tony Hawk board is 'Fine'? Seriously?" Joe asks looking at the side of my head for a hole.

"No, it is sweet. It's amazing, actually. Sorry, I didn't mean to sound ungrateful or whatever, it's just –"

"Just what? Is there something wrong with it? Is there something wrong with you?" Joe's looking at me funny now.

"No, there's nothing wrong with the board. It's perfect. There might be something wrong with me though," I mumble.

"Wrong with you? What? What could be wrong with a dude who's about to kick some serious ass at the Westside Skateboard Invitational?"

"Well, not wrong, really. It's just that – well – I'm nervous. Super nervous. I wasn't yesterday or all week, but now that it's so close, I can't help thinking that I'm going to completely choke and I really want you all to be proud of me. You all got me this crazy amazing board and have been helping me out, I just don't want to screw it up," I blurt out.

"Are you thanking me?" Joe asks, smiling.

"I guess I am. Thanks. And I also really don't want to screw this up."

"You won't," Joe says like there's no other option.

"Just like that? I won't?"

"Right. Just like that. You'll kick butt. The end," Joe says, not a doubt in his voice.

"Thanks for helping me out, Joe. I'm going to go practice kicking some butt now," I say and smile.

"You do that," Joe says and heads back inside. "It's a team effort, kid. No one does anything in this world by himself," Joe says right before the door closes.

Right after the door closes, Wheeler, Grinder, and Vert skate by. "See you on the half-pipe, Loser," Wheeler says as he flies past.

"Yeah, Loser!" Vert adds.

I don't say anything. It's not worth it. I go back to skating, just sort of circling around the lot thinking about what Joe said, about the Invitational, about my mom when I hear, "Hey, are you gonna do something or just roll around?" It's Jen and she's smiling.

"Oh, hey," I say and stop.

"Oh, no, don't let me stop you. I just wanted to say 'Hi' on my way home. Think you're ready?"

"Well, I guess. Ready as I'll ever be," I admit.

"Just concentrate on what you're doing. You'll be fine. No, wait, scratch that. You'll be great," Jen says smiling.

I laugh and ask "How do you know I'll be so great?"

"I just know," she says. "Gotta go. See you tomorrow at the Invitational!" and she's gone.

I watch her walk away, wave one more time as she turns the corner and then I circle around the lot gaining speed. One more time on the half-pipe and then I'm done. Whatever happens I decide. I swing my leg high and fly up the half-pipe. I know I've heard this a thousand times before, but it really is amazing how much easier something can get with practice. I leave the lot confident, almost positive I'll do good tomorrow. I hope.

The Westside Skate Park is packed. Kids from all the middle and high schools around are there. There are tons of people I don't recognize. As soon as I get there I scope out the crowd to find Jen and my mom and Ms. James. They're all sitting together about halfway up the bleachers. I wave, but they don't see me.

I was supposed to be there 45 minutes before my competition started, but I get there extra early mostly because I couldn't stand to sit at home any longer. I watch the younger, mostly more beginning kids compete. There are a couple of bad falls, some tears even, but mostly there are no surprises about which kids win and which kids don't. Then the announcer bellows, "The competition will now move on to the advanced skateboarders. Advanced skateboarders will be judged on a three-point system for each of the three events: Street, Vert, and Freestyle." My nerves are starting to rev up, but I feel weirdly calm, like this is no big deal. The announcer then says, "Our judges for tonight need no introduction to the skate world. Please welcome Ryan Schklar, Chad Muska, and Stavro Niarchos." The crowd goes nuts, and so do I. Now I really do feel nervous. "Competitors, you will begin in five minutes! Let the competition begin!" the announcer screams and just as I got really nervous really quickly, I now feel weirdly calm, like I'm in my own sort of bubble. I'm here to skate and I'll skate. I'll skate really well. I don't know how I know this, I just know.

CHAPTER EIGHTEEN

I sit there in my bubble watching about ten skaters go through their moves. They're all good, no doubt. Then it's Wheeler's turn. For once, I really don't care that he's there. Not even Wheeler can bug me today. For once I'm not looking for a place to hide in case he sees me and wants to call me a loser again. I don't care anymore what he thinks of me. Wheeler is really good too, and he almost makes it to the end flawlessly. Right at the end though, he wobbles on a landing and almost falls. The judges give him a 222 – a great score, but not perfect. I'm up. I don't think much, I just go. I can't hear the crowd at all. I'm just doing my thing. In the zone, thinking, I love skating. I'm just here to have a good time. I only think of my landings for half a second before I go to the next jump. Mostly I'm thinking "Sweet! Nailed it," and then I'm skating to the next move. It's fun. I'm just having fun. It doesn't feel like I'm competing at all. Finally I roll to a stop, hop off the park floor and look at the judges: 333. Then I go nuts, and so does everyone else.

"Ladies and Gentlemen, we will take a ten minute break before the next event, Vert," the announcer says and I look around for my water bottle.

Jen's smiling ear to ear when she finally gets my attention. "Hey! Chris! Chris!" She's come down to the side of the park floor right across from where I'm sitting. I smile and wave back, but I've got some business to take care of. "Hey! My wheels are loose. I'm going to go get them tightened," I yell, but I'm not sure she hears me. "I'll talk to you after, ok?"

"Ok! You're doing awesome! I'm so proud of you!" Jen yells and then heads back up to where she was sitting.

I smile and yell "Thanks!" and then head over to the repair

counter. Shido's there looking super busy like he's the host to the biggest party in the state.

"Hey, pretty good skating out there," Shido says barely looking up.

"Thanks. Hey, can you tighten the rear wheels a little?" I ask, putting my board on the counter.

"No prob. Take just a sec. I gotta do these first." There are two other boards on the counter lined up. I'm not worried. I figure I got at least 30 minutes until I skate again.

Just as I turn around this little kid shoves a notebook and a pen in my gut and says "Can I have your autograph?"

"Huh?" For a second I think I might punch this kid who just shoved me, but then I realize what he's asking for.

"Your autograph! Will you sign this paper? My name's Jason. You were awesome out there, really amazing," the kid says jumping up and down waiting for me to sign.

"Sure, kid. I'll sign it. 'Jason' you said?"

"Yeah, Jason. I skate too. Next year I'm going to compete. My mom says she might get me a better board for my birthday. The one I got now's pretty crummy, but I practice anyhow. I'm working on an ollie right now. Almost landed it twice," the kid says talking a mile a minute.

"Well, that's great. Uh, keep practicing. You'll get better. I promise," I tell him feeling weird, like I'm suddenly an adult giving out advice to kids. It's weird, but it's pretty cool too.

"You're going to win, I know it," the kid says taking back his pen and paper.

"Well, the competition's not over yet. There's still two more events to go."

"Yeah, well, I think you're going to win. You're the best. Thanks!" he says and disappears back up the bleachers.

"Hey, thank you," I say.

    The Vert competition starts. All of the skaters up until Wheeler fall or wobble. It's sort of a disaster of an event until Wheeler skates. He skates flawlessly and gets himself a perfect 333. I glance over at Joe who, as my sponsor, is sitting behind me. We've hardly talked at all today. Joe's been keeping his distance. "No offense kid, but I just can't talk to you today. You look like you're in the zone and I get that, I really do. It used to happen to me. I'm definitely not in the zone, so I'm staying away. I don't want to ruin your mojo," Joe said real fast right before the advanced events started.

"Fine by me. Do what you gotta do, Joe," I told him. I honestly forgot that he was behind me until I heard him swear under his breath when Wheeler's Vert score was shown.

"You all right?" I ask Joe, half laughing. He's a mess. His hair is all crazy from running his hands through it, he's twisted his program into a tight rope and his legs are both bouncing like he's got springs on his shoes.

"Just ducky, kid, ducky. Hey! Don't look at me! Keep your head in the game! You're next," Joe practically yells at me.

"I know. I got it. I got this," I tell him smiling and I head out.

Just like before, everything is going great, perfect in fact, until I'm on my way up the last half-pipe and my board stops and I go flying into the rail. It takes me a second to understand what's happened. My board is rolling toward me at the bottom of the half-pipe, the crowd is muttering, and I see Joe start to head my way. I'm not hurt, just really surprised. I didn't mess up a landing, I lost my board on the way up. That only happens to complete amateurs.

"No! You can't go out there! You can't help him. He's got to finish the course," I hear Jen yell, and she's right. I have to finish or I'll be disqualified from the competition. I know Joe knows this, but he runs back to the sides almost as quickly as he ran out. Just sort of a knee jerk reaction I guess. I get up and notice the blood on my shirt from my nose. I guess I am hurt. I get back on my board and suddenly I hear the crowd. They're whistling and clapping, screaming like maniacs. I finish the course, and head toward Joe. I'm more confused than hurt, and then suddenly I'm mad, really mad. The only way that I could have screwed up that set up is if my board was messed up. But it's a brand new board and I have been the only one to use it or even touch it until today, until right before I went out on the floor for the Vert event. I throw my helmet on the ground and toss my board after it.

"It's ok, Chris. You'll get 'em next time," I hear Jen say. She's run down to the side again. Jen's the best, but right now, I'm not in the mood for encouragement.

"What the hell happened out there? Here." Joe hands me a towel and Jen moves like she's going to help me clean up, but then she changes her mind. "There's something wrong with your board, isn't there?" Joe says real quiet and then he picks it up and looks at the wheels. "Yep, something's definitely not right here," Joe says spinning the back wheels.

"Someone definitely messed up my board. I just had the wheels tightened right before the Vert. It had to have happened then, but who did it? Shido? Why would he do that?" I say real fast to Joe.

"There's really no way to prove that someone messed with it or who messed with it. It's dirty, that's for sure, but it wouldn't be the first time someone played dirty at an Invitational. But, yes someone has messed with the wheels and yes, whoever that is is a complete loser," Joe says, pulling his truck tool out of his pocket.

"It's my own stupid fault. I should've checked them before I went out," I say and sit down on the bench. I hear the crowd moan as my score is shown: 121. "Well, I guess that's it."

"No it ain't."

"There's no way. I can't win."

Joe has nothing to say to that because he knows I'm right, so there's a really awkward silence until Jen says, "Do you have to?"

"Do I have to? Have to what?" I ask.

"Win. Do you have to win? I mean, is that why you're competing? To win?"

"Well, I guess I originally said that that really wasn't why I was competing..." I say, remembering.

Then my mom and Ms. James show up next to Jen. "Chris, are you ok? What happened?" My mom hates blood, I know, so I smile to show her I'm fine.

"Someone's messed with his board," says Joe who hands my board back to me.

"You're kidding," Ms. James says.

"Nope, not kidding," Joe answers.

"But didn't you just fix it?" Jen asks.

"Nope. Can't. The wheel axle is cracked," Joe says shrugging.

Then I have an answer: "No, I don't have to."

"Huh?" Joe says looking at me like I've lost it.

"Jen, you asked me if I had to win. And the answer is no, I don't have to. But I'm gonna finish."

Joe reaches around to his duffle bag and pulls out his gold and silver skateboard. "You'll need a board," he says.

"No way. You brought your board? Why?"

"You never know. Now it's your board," he says and hands it

to me.

"Are you serious?"

"As a heart attack. Besides. How could you finish without a board? What were you going to do – try it in your socks?" Joe laughs.

"Thanks," I say.

"Ladies and Gentlemen, the third and final category, Freestyle, will begin in 10 minutes," the announcer says.

"We should get back to our seats," Ms. James says looking at my mom and Jen.

"Ok," Jen says, "Good luck, Chris! You'll do great even if you don't win."

"Knock 'em dead Chris!" my mom bellows, shooting her fists up in the air, which really cracks me up.

"You got it, Mom," I say and sit back down to wait for my turn.

CHAPTER NINETEEN

The final category, Freestyle, begins. This is where we really get to show off, at least according to Joe. "It was my favorite – the one I looked forward to most," Joe told me one day at the lot. "You know, you get this great idea for a jump and you know you've never seen anyone do it but you, or you're the one who showed it to your buddies. For Freestyle you get to show it to everyone. Like it's the debut of your original move, you know?"

"Yeah, I get it," I told him. "Like this is the category where you get to show everyone that you're not like every other skater out there. Like you're an inventor too or choreographer or whatever you'd call it," I said.

"Right. A mad scientist on wheels," Joe grinned and made a crazy mad scientist face.

The first few kids do all right. I have seen some of their moves before. It's kind of hard to keep new stuff quiet in the skating world. There are some moves I haven't seen before, but nothing that's really amazing. Then it's Wheeler's turn. Wheeler starts off kind of shaky, which is surprising, but he finishes really well. He manages to make me say "Wow," with a flip spin that is impressive, but, I gotta say, not new.

"I need all 3s to win, don't I," I turn and ask Joe.

"Depends on how Wheeler does. And that's if you want to tie, Buddy," Joe says watching Wheeler. "Who knows though, maybe you'll be the first skater to score a perfect 4."

"Yeah, right," I say to Joe who is not laughing at all.

"Never know," Joe says. "I say just have fun. Go out there like it doesn't matter, like there are no numbers attached to how you do, cuz, when all's said and done – do the numbers really matter? Skating's for the rebels, Dude, the kids who invented surfing on concrete. Sometimes I wonder why we even have Invitationals, you know? Like, tell me exactly how going to an Invitational with judges, scores, rules, categories is at all like skating should be," Joe's looking right at me now, very serious.

"What? You're the one who convinced me, no begged, made me do this!"

"Yeah, well. It's still a good idea to get your name out there. But just have fun ok? Heads up. You're on," Joe says and is back looking at the arena.

"Sometimes, Joe, I tell you…" I say, laughing. Joe always keeps me on my toes, that's for sure. What a guy.

"Just have fun, ok?" Joe says.

"That's what I'm planning on," I smile and take off. Knowing that there's no way I can win takes all the pressure off. So I have fun – a lot of fun. Maybe Joe's right: skating's about originality, not doing what everyone else is doing. It doesn't matter that I can't win, so why not just do it the way I, me, Chris Reynolds, would do it if nothing was riding on it? I trash the routine Joe and I worked on and head toward the 12 foot pipe, full on. I've pictured this a thousand times, and there's no doubt in my mind about how to do it. I know that I can do it, now it's just a question of how much fun can I have doing it.

"Here goes nothing," I say to myself when I approach the pipe, as fast as I've ever gone. And then I think to myself: This one's for Jen. I'm up, I'm airborne for what seems like forever, I bend, I got my board in hand, I twist around and snap my legs back under the board. Everything just feels perfect, easy, almost like my body and the board and the pipe were built for this. As soon as I land I want to do it again, but then I hear the crowd. They are the loudest they've been all day. I skate around, looking in the bleachers for Jen, but I can't quite spot her, so

129

I build up my speed again and well, I figure, that worked out well, so I go for another Monkey Flip and, it's even higher, and I hang in the air even longer and I twist I little harder on the way back to my board. It's the most amazing feeling I've ever had on my board, and I know I'm grinning like an idiot on my way back to the bottom of the pipe. I do some more tricks, good ones. Variations on ollies and kick flips that might be original to me, I'm not really sure, and then I'm done and I skate to the side and off the floor to where Joe's is standing with his mouth hanging open.

"What the hell was that? That was incredible! Is that the thing you were trying to land at the lot? Was that it?" Joe is now yelling and shaking me, smiling and pointing and shaking me some more.

"Dude! Calm down! You're gonna shake my head off!"

"Calm down? I can't calm down! That was amazing. I wish you could have seen it. It was like you were hanging from a wire up there! You made it look so easy, like it was nothing. Awesome!" Joe is genuinely nuts right now. Jumping, yelling, shooting his fists in the air.

I look from Joe to the bleachers to try and find Jen again and I see her, her and my mom and Ms. James. They're all jumping up and down hugging each other and yelling something I can't hear. And then I see Jen see me and she's smiling huge and shakes her head and mouths "Monkey Flip," and I nod and mouth back "Monkey Flip."

I'm grinning ear to ear, wondering if I can do it again. I look over to the judges who at first raise 332, but then the crowd moans and the last card holder looks at the card, shakes his head, and changes it to a 3. The crowd roars their approval.

At the award ceremony about an hour later, both Wheeler and

I are on the platform, each of us holding the first place trophy.

"Well fans, it looks like we don't have enough of the right kind of trophy here. We'll just have to get another!" The announcer sounds corny, but I don't care. Now Wheeler's holding the trophy, but then he sort of hands it to me. I put my hand on it, but Wheeler doesn't let go. We both hold it up high and the crowd goes wild.

CHAPTER TWENTY

After about a week, the hype about Wheeler and me tying for first place dies down at school, and everything more or less goes back to normal. Amazingly there's even a moment leaving the cafeteria when Wheeler spots me, comes over and says, "You gotta show me that Monkey Flip some time, Reynolds. It looks like a blast."

"Yeah, it is. No problem. Name the time and place," I answer. No real plans are made, but I think it's pretty amazing that Wheeler doesn't end the conversation with "Loser" or "Moron."

There's just two weeks left of school and the Spring Poetry Fest is here. I had heard about the Spring Poetry Fest basically since the year began, so I had a pretty good idea that this Fest was a really big deal at Warren Middle. Mr. Hess is of course in his glory for the last couple of weeks helping kids pick poems to read at the Fest and helping the poets polish their own poems to be read. The closer we get to the Fest date, the happier and more intense Mr. Hess gets. Rehearsals are held in the auditorium for the last week before the Fest, so all of Mr. Hess' classes sit in the seats while kid after kid practices walking on stage without tripping, talking into the microphone without blowing anybody's ears out, waiting for applause, and then walking back off stage without falling down the four stairs.

"Thank you, Lindsay, well done. I'm sure your parents will be very proud," Mr. Hess tells Lindsay who of course has written an amazing poem about spring and new beginnings.

"And next, let's see, ah yes, Mr. Robert Frost's 'The Trial by Existence,' which will be recited by Christopher Reynolds," Mr. Hess says flipping through pages of notes.

I get up and am way more nervous than I was at any

point during the Invitational. "Just have fun," I remember Joe saying. Fun? I think to myself. How exactly is this fun? Try to enjoy it maybe. I picked the poem because I like it, so maybe that's what I need to do here, enjoy it. I've made it up the stage and to the microphone without tripping. "My name is Chris Reynolds and I will be reading 'Trial by Existence' by Robert Frost," I say into the microphone. There's no squealing feedback and I haven't made anyone cover their ears. I look up take a deep breath and begin.

———————

"Mom? Moooom!! Mom! Did you iron my shirt?" I yell from my bedroom. I know she hates it when I yell for her without actually coming to look for her first. I also know that she won't answer even if she hears me, but I forget all this because my nerves are shot and I got about ten minutes until I'm supposed to be at school in the auditorium sitting with my class.

"Chris, I hear you," my mom says very calmly. "I was walking up the stairs to give you your just ironed shirt," she says. Lucky for me she's not mad. "I can see you're a little nervous," she says smiling.

"Ugh. Yes. I hate being nervous," I say and put the shirt on.

"I don't think anyone likes it, but it's not like you have no experience being nervous."

"What do you mean?" I ask.

"At the Invitational? About three weeks ago? Don't tell me you weren't nervous," my mom says.

"Weirdly I wasn't that nervous," I say trying to get the top button to button.

"Oh, come on."

"No, seriously. It's like I knew that I should be nervous, but I just couldn't get all jumpy. I was excited for sure, but not really nervous. It's like I knew what I was doing, you know? And I knew that even if I completely screwed up, it wouldn't be that bad."

"Well, you can think of tonight like that then," my mom says handing me my tie.

"No, this is different. I can totally screw this up. Royally. I've always been good at skating, even the first time I got on a board. I just understand skating. It's easy for me, but reading and reading out loud in front of tons of people? Not so great at that. Terrible, in fact" I say.

"Well, I think you'll be just fine. No, better than fine. I think you'll be terrific," Mom says smiling and straightening my tie.

"You're supposed to think that. You're my mom," I say and manage a small smile.

"Come on, we don't want to screw up by being late," Mom says and she heads out.

Just before I hit the lights I spot my dad's photo on the dresser. I'm not exactly sure why, but I walk over and grab the poem of his that's my favorite that I keep right behind the picture, shove it in my pocket and then I turn out the lights and take the stairs two at a time.

———

I'm in the seats with Jen and the others who have already done their thing. The place is packed. It looks like it's not just everyone's parents, but grandparents, aunts, uncles and cousins are all there. I guess they weren't kidding when they said the whole town looks forward to Warren's Spring Poetry Fest, "The 72 year tradition."

Jen looks at me, whispers "Wish me luck!" and crosses her fingers.

"You don't need luck. You'll be awesome!" I whisper back. Jen rolls her eyes and we both laugh and then she heads out onto the stage. She reads a poem by Emily Dickenson that she spent about an hour explaining to me one day after school. She of course is flawless and gets huge applause and even some hoots.

A lot has changed since the beginning of the year, but I am still not one of Mr. Hess' favorite students. Like the Invitational, I know I'm not going to 'win' this Poetry Fest, because it's not really a competition, but I decide I'm going to try have fun, or at least enjoy it as much as I can. I pull out my dad's poem and look it over one more time before I hear Mr. Hess say "Next we have Mr. Chris Reynolds."

There's some clapping as I get to the microphone, but most of the clapping is for after the reading, so it feels a little awkward walking up there in the relative quiet. "I was planning to do 'The Trial by Existence' by Robert Frost, but I found a poem I liked better." I look up at the audience who makes no noise and I try really hard not to think about the face Mr. Hess must be making right now. "I will recite a poem my father wrote." I see my mom in the second row looking really nervous. "You see, he, my dad, thought he was a failure, and maybe some other people thought he was too. But he left me something that's really important to me, so you could say that he wasn't a failure at all. Not everyone is remembered for something they've created, something original that's theirs alone, but my dad is, and to me, that's the furthest thing from a failure there is. This poem is called 'Suppose' by William R. Reynolds." I clear my throat and begin:

'Suppose that some gifts come without reason.
Flying nightly into our bedrooms,
Whispering sweetly into our ears,
Kissing our eyelids.

And dancing with our dreams.
In that deepest hell of night...
Can we find the strength to grasp
That gossamer thread of hope
So thin, pale, and fragile?
But suppose someone shakes us to say
Thank you.'"

It's really quiet when I finish. I find my mom in the crowd again and could see that she was half smiling and half crying. And then people start to applaud, slowly at first. There aren't cheers or hoots or any "Bravo!"s, but more and more people start to clap.

"Thank you, Mr. Reynolds. A moving poem, certainly," Mr. Hess says, and then I fold the paper and walk back off stage, back to my seat next to Jen.

"That was beautiful," Jen says when I get back to my seat. She has a huge smile on her face. "You were perfect!"

"I don't know about perfect, but I think it went pretty well," I whisper back. "You think Hess'll kill me?"

"Well, maybe not kill, but let's just say you two aren't ever going to be buddy buddy," Jen says laughing.

"I figured that," I say laughing back. I sit back and watch the other kids recite their poems and start thinking that this year has been a year I never would have predicted. I never thought I'd skate in an Invitational, I never thought I'd get Wheeler off my back, I never thought the prettiest and nicest girl in school would like me and I absolutely never ever thought I would be able to get up in front of a crowd of people and recite a poem without screwing up all the words. And then I thought: the thing that seems the same in all this is that I was myself for all of it. I didn't try to be anyone else. I tried to have fun, I tried to do it the way I wanted to do it, and maybe that was the key. Like the song says "I did it my way." And then it suddenly occurs to me: my dad taught me that. With his poetry and his never ending belief in his ability to be a poet no matter what anyone said, he taught me that.

About Kathy Garrett

Kathy is a freelance writer who has published poetry and several academic essays in a number of journals. She also teaches writing and literature at the College for Creative Studies in Detroit. Her two sons, who spend a lot of time on skateboards, helped her with his project.

About Brian Webster

Brian is dyslexic. He sees his dyslexia as a gift for coming up with his story ideas. He has turned these ideas into several screenplays, two of which won awards at the Moondance International Film Festival and another was a finalist in a Holiday Screenplay contest. He has also coauthored two adult books, Death by Default and Bundle of Hope. His children's books include: *Snowville, Santa's Elf, Trapped in Toyland,* and *Model Kid. Monkey Flip* is Brian's first Young Adult Reader. He has also written a screenplay based on this book. Brian lives with his wife, Cathy, in Canton, MI. Their blended family includes five adult children and one grandchild.

Acknowledgements

A big thank you to my stepson, Michael Bosman for his cover design and to photographer, Glenn Yeager, for his expertise. Thanks to Kris Yankee for her careful editing, Gwen Frederickson for the layout and Tim Trinka who coordinated the publishing.

Finally my heartfelt thanks go to my wife Cathy for her support and encouragement along with my family who continues to provide inspiration for my stories.